LIFE IS A BUTT DIAL
TALES FROM A LIFE AMONG THE TRAGICALLY HIP

BY

CLEVE HATTERSLEY

LIFE IS A BUTT DIAL
TALES FROM A LIFE AMONG THE TRAGICALLY HIP

by
Cleve Hattersley

Illustrations by
Cleve Hattersley

Edited by
Craig Hattersley

© 2019 by Cleve Marshall Hattersley. All rights reserved. No part of this book may be reproduced or transmitted in any form or by any means, electronic, mechanical, photocopying, recording, or otherwise, without the express written permission of the author.

Library of Congress Control Number: 2019909911

ISBN 978-1-7336383-1-9 (print)
ISBN 978-1-7336383-2-6 (e-book)

Foreword

The author of this book, Cleve Hattersley, is a man who is very well adjusted to a sick society. I've known Cleve since Christ was a cowboy, and he does not appear to be getting any more emotionally or spiritually stable than he was back then, which is to say he has, if anything, maintained his heroic stance living on the edge of life. Perhaps because of this, he has written an oddly compelling, very funny, and quite often very brilliant book.

But *Life Is a Butt Dial* is not entirely a romance novel; the book is as nonfiction as it gets, still hanging on to the hopes and dreams of its fascinating and fucked-up characters. Some are dead and some are living, but in Cleve's life he's met them all. Yet *Butt Dial* avoids the mandatory fugue of celebrity name-dropping. They're all present and accounted for, but Cleve takes them on with a withering, if not to say jaundiced, eye. Hattersley evidently agrees with Hemingway: "Fame is death's little sister."

Cleve Hattersley pioneered the seminal rock group, Greezy Wheels. He also managed the Lone Star Cafe in New York during its bold, beautiful, ball-busting heyday. Few people indeed have Cleve's insights into music and the music business. Groucho Marx once told me in a men's room in New York, "I've met everybody I want to meet." Cleve, I'm fairly certain, feels pretty much the same way. I'm not sure, however, if he's ever met Groucho Marx in a men's room.

So I highly recommend reading *Life Is a Butt Dial*. Read it for the voice. Read it for the history. Read it for the memories.

Those are three good reasons to buy any book.

—Kinky Friedman

You can call it Fate, you can call it Karma

Or you can enter the twenty-first century and call it what it is—a butt dial. In my lifetime, I've seen cursive handwriting reduced to block-letter printing to fonts to the forthcoming dominant form of communication, the emoji. Soon, publishing companies will send me little pictures of piles of shit instead of rejection notices. Oh yay.

We call it butt dial because . . . well, that's what it is. You sit on or brush over your "device" and it dials someone else's "device." We call 'em devices because they are no longer phones—they are our closest companions. It is merely unfortunate that the closest companion to about half the fucking planet is named Siri. At any rate, it was an event not planned; you had no intention or need to speak to your friend, nor he/she to you. It was the device doing the deciding. The devices are now our oracles.

The oracle in my life has surprised me at every turn. Whereas most oracles speak a kind of truth, mine lies like a motherfucker. When it tells me I'm happening, I'm clearly not. When I think I'm happening, it tells me I am not. When

I once pondered a future as a shrink, my oracle said, "Good plan." When I smoked my first joint, it said, "Bad idea." Of course, after I finished that first joint, it said: "My bad. Good plan." Sometimes it can't help but tell the truth.

But I was never really meant to be a shrink. I was just a great candidate—in other words, a total psycho mess. As is every shrink I have ever met. Psychiatry ultimately just wasn't in me. I have a hard time shutting up, an even harder time listening, and my tendency to flit from subject to subject with very little substance disqualifies me from a position that requires digging carefully though a patient's brain over years and years, at an extremely high cost to that patient.

I ended up falling into the music business, wherein flitting is encouraged (we call it noodling), and everyone is just about the same psycho mess as the psychiatrists. We know this because the drugs invented by the psychiatrists became musician staples. I also took a side trip through politics that forced me to look through voters' brains, at an extremely high cost to myself.

Very few of my choices were actual decisions. They were more like resignations, resignations to the limits on my previously chosen paths. In other words, Fate driven. Karma inspired. Butt-dialed. I pretty much followed the lead of a guy called Sad Sack, a WWII cartoon character created by George Baker for Harvey Comics. The way Sad Sack decided which road to take at a junction was to spit in his hand, slap both hands together, and go whichever direction the spit came out.

Just like a butt dial. Except the spit was the oracle.

Every day is a blinding toad

Okay, I'll go with winding road, but aren't the two pretty much the same—the unforeseen in life? Or butt dials? How else can I explain that I am here writing this drivel after having survived a life filled with roads, toads, and butt dials? Yes, I'm writing this book about it, but the real reward here is that I have both survived and inspired personal memories in others. I believe everyone has experienced a blinding toad or two in life.

How else did I end up at the Night Owl Cafe in NYC in the mid-Sixties, except that I stumbled into it in my desperate attempt to cleanse myself of a possible swamp-dwelling career in advertising? I had imagined being a giant in the advertising business, selling cars, perfumes, and cheeseburgers to an unsuspecting populace. Turns out I was a giant douche for even imagining such a thing. Seeing the toll creative lying took on the martini and dexedrine-fueled execs on the eleventh floor at J. Walter Thompson, and imagining what horrors were being committed on consumers, I quickly opted for a reality check.

I went south, downtown Manhattan. While I wouldn't exactly describe the Village (Greenwich, of course) as a reality check, it was my new reality, the reality I have carried through life, and the reality I continue to occupy. At that time, the Village was the acknowledged center of the universe, and I needed to be there. It has always been my desire to be at the center of shit. Not sure why—must be some sort of magnetism or gravity. Or magic.

But, wow, the Village in the Sixties! Hip-hugging bell-bottoms, polka dots, Beatle boots, beautiful girls in awesome miniskirts, bagel babies, fringe, teeny boppers . . . and hair (I did not get another haircut for the next nine years)—all in a fantastical promenade up and down Bleecker, MacDougal, and West Third streets. Little musical paradises were everywhere, but I wandered into the first decent one I saw as I left the subway and walked west on Third. That was the Night Owl Cafe. I knew nothing about it.

I soon did, and I fucking loved the place. I went to so many shows (and paid so many covers), Joe Mara, the beefy Italian who owned the place, started letting me hang for free and fill in for his doorman, Jack the Rat, who led a life tenuously strung between beatnik and that guy who tries to clean your windshield with a filthy spit rag. We were never sure when he'd make it to work. The doorman was the shill, considered a necessity to compete. I found shill a much more rewarding and freeing profession than ad weasel. I would patter endlessly to passersby. Got paid five bucks a night to develop that patter into what would later become my stage persona—that annoying, obnoxious loudmouth who never shuts the fuck up.

And I got to see every show. Tim Hardin, so messed

up he could barely stand up, yet crooning some of the most haunting (and perfectly performed) tunes ever written. Richie Havens, before he had his front teeth replaced. James Taylor, in all his pain-in-the-ass smarm, fronting the Flying Machine with Danny Kortchmar. Gram Parsons, my first pure country-rock experience, the International Submarine Band (liked him, wasn't crazy about the genre). The Allman Joy, the antithesis of the Carnaby Street-ness of the MacDougal nexus—they all looked like savages. But holy shit, that guitar guy!

There was one player who didn't get the gig there, even though he was blowing it up big down the street. I was having a cup of coffee one afternoon, admiring a couple of the cuter miniskirted British wannabes who regularly patrolled the club, when the most colorful single individual I had ever seen came in with his guitar strapped over his shoulder. Peter Max could have painted his ensemble, and he had a smile that just floored you. Or at least it floored me. I don't think the miniskirt wannabes even noticed. He wasn't exactly their ideal Brit lookalike. He was black. And he didn't look a bit like Mick Jagger.

He was Jimi Hendrix. I didn't know this at the time, as he was billing himself as Jimmy James and the Blue Flames down the street at the Cafe Wha. He plugged into the house amp and started playing solo. I don't remember what he was playing—blown mind plus fifty years have obscured that—but it was beyond question the most astounding audition I have ever witnessed. He did every trick for which he later became a god, including playing with his teeth and behind his back. And what he played was quite obviously the beginning of the revolution. Amazing, transcendent melodies and astonishing noodles filled the almost empty sixty-seat room. He did all this *left-handed*. When he finished, I fairly bubbled up to the stage to . . . I dunno . . . give him head maybe? Yeah, I probably would have, too.

I cannot clearly convey how astonished I was when Joe turned Jimi down for the gig. I thought I was the one doing drugs. Had he been watching the same show? Was there some sort of racist overtone here? Come to think of it, I don't recall any other black performers/bands at the Night Owl other than Richie, and Joe was, after all, a *goombah* in a *goombah* neighborhood. I never blamed Joe for such things, and I have only recently heard that to this day, Joe, alive and well in the old neighborhood, still considers turning Jimi down one of the worst mistakes of his life. Sorry, Joe, I concur, but I understand.

Nah, I still don't understand.

Cafe Wha got the glory when Chas Chandler, who had been hanging at the Night Owl nightly with Eric Burden, caught Jimi's act there just a couple months later and whisked him off to England. The Wha is still there. I believe the Night Owl is now a Japanese Restaurant. Thank you, Joe Mara, for one of the top three best blinding toads of my life.

Nothing beats a grand entrance for getting someone's attention

Coming in strong will bring people forward in their seats, engage them fully. It will allow you to do and be exactly what you want to do or be. Of course, if the rest of your performance is dog shit, you may regret having spent half your budget on that fucking grand entrance. You must then ponder: Be I doing this shit right?

Perhaps the ultimate grand entrance of my era (the Stone Age) was created by Arthur Brown, as in "The Crazy World of . . ." Arthur broke out in 1968, and one of his earliest American shows was at the Fillmore East. His big hit was "Fire," a song about . . . fire. And he was plenty serious about flames, having nearly self-immolated three times by the time he hit the Fillmore. As I later learned upon meeting him and being asked to help him with his memoirs, this fire fascination may have baked him more than just a bit.

For his grand entrance at his premier Fillmore show, he was carried to the stage on a sedan chair by six rather handsome young men, all shirtless, who may or may not have lived somewhere around Sheridan Square. The four corners of the chair featured tiki torches, fully ablaze and dangerously spewing hot ashes to either side of the aisle. Yes, Arthur was conveyed to the stage on a burning four-poster bed.

The thing is, I remember absolutely nothing about the show. Because there wasn't much to remember. There was makeup, there were histrionics, and there was plenty o' pomp. Just not a lot of good music. I like a musical show to have good music. Nevertheless, Arthur influenced everyone from Alice Cooper to Marilyn Manson with all that pomp and lack of circumspect. If someone would let him back in, I bet he'd enter in flames.

The entrance is everything in life, as well as on stage. My next two fave grand arrivals occurred in real time, not stage time. Both were awe inspiring, though one was a good 'un and one was a bad 'un. You always hope for the good 'uns, pray against the bad 'uns, and often settle for the so-so 'uns.

One of Kinky's all-time grand entrances would be a list-topper in anyone's annals. I just wish more people had witnessed it, other than the New York Rangers and their wives, upon whom Kinky laid his grandness. I believe I was the only other person who saw this most exquisite entry.

The Rangers, who had just won a Stanley Cup or something (not a hockey fan here), had become regulars at the Lone Star Cafe. Larry "Ratso" Sloman had intro'd them to Kinky and the club. Ratso wrote a book about the Rangers called *Thin Ice*. Ratso is a hockey fan. I think he just likes hockey masks. Rats does have some weird tastes, though, many of them currently on display in his preference for day-glo orange suits.

On this night, most of the team was seated with their wives in the back of the club. They were all dressed to the nines. I had never seen the guys so dolled up. Hockey players are a rough bunch. You expected to see them looking like the lumberjacks they might have become had they not discovered they could make bucks and have fun skating fast and knocking the shit out of each other. But they were rocking tuxes, and their wives were resplendent in obviously expensive evening wear.

I'm pretty sure Kinky did not get the memo. Either that or he had christened as dinner wear the extra large hockey jersey and cowboy boots he was wearing. At least he hadn't showed up wearing uncreased jeans, a major faux pas to our general manager, Don Reynolds. He wasn't wearing any visible pants at all. Much better.

He was a good six or eight sheets to the wind and marching like a motherfucker. Two white rings under his nose proved he'd gotten the marching orders several hours prior. On the way to the back of the club, where the dinner party had already run most of its course, he grabbed a Lone Star from one of the bartenders, took two large gulps, put his thumb over it and started shaking it vigorously. Yeah, this didn't look good.

Kinky walked straight up to the table and sprayed the entire team and all the wives with Lone Star beer. One of the guys, I think it was Nick Fotiu, saw Kinky coming, but he couldn't act fast enough to do anything. I see it all now in slow motion: Kinky heading for disaster, Nick standing up to try to stop him, and suds hitting nearly everyone in the face. Wow, what an entrance!

I have no idea why the guys almost instantly forgave Kinky for "being Kinky," but I did have a good idea what they were going to hear from their wives at home, judging by the looks of fury on every woman's face. I suppose I could have prevented this grandest of arrivals, but why would I take that away from Kinky?

My personal fave grand entrance was one of my own. First, I must stipulate that I am a Yankee, born and raised in New York, but please, I am not a carpetbagger. I like hardwood floors, have never been a carpet fan. Saltillo tiles? Maybe. No, I am a NY Yankee, as in pinstripes and The Mick. I was born into it, on Mickey Mantle's birthday in fact. Hate me now, if you must. I am not responsible for . . . myself.

My pal Stephen and our other friend named Steve actually tried out for the Yankees, both having been bred in the city. I could only watch from upstate and collect baseball cards. If only I had been a bit more careful with some of those cards, I wouldn't be trying to whore myself out as a writer today.

Of the three of us buds, though, I was the one who actually made buds with Yankees. There are some tales to tell here, but we shall skip to this chase. Hey, it's my fucking grand entrance. Anyway, Goose Gossage was my closest pal. I first met him when he was teasing Bad Billy, our ex-prizefighter bouncer at the Lone Star. Billy was as tough and as damaged a man as anyone I've ever met. His face was one big cauliflower, with a slalom-shaped nose, and to say he was a bit punch drunk was a high compliment.

I persuaded Goose that maybe, just maybe, Billy could seriously hurt him. Goose never actually allowed this would happen—he was a big ole country boy after all—but he backed off, and we struck it off immediately. We quickly developed a deal in which either of us could call ahead for tickets to either games or shows. Goose, Billy Martin, Greg Nettles, Tommy John, Oscar Gamble, pretty much the whole team except Reggie came down to the club. This meant I could ask virtually all of them for passes if I wanted to bring a crowd to the game. And of course, I wanted to bring a crowd to the game. I don't think I ever took fewer than twenty folks with me to any one game. We always sat in the players' wives' section, behind home plate, where I became known as the asshole who never stopped shouting, "Pitcher's got a rag arm!"

On most occasions I'd stop at the dugout with a shout-out to the guys. One time I took them all Lone Star Cafe t-shirts, which they all promptly put on after the game. Worn logo shirts meant good promo. Mort understood this. His partner Bill, not so much. Mort credited me with developing high-profile clients. Bill credited me with a bill for the shirts.

I credited myself for not paying it.

On the day of my grand entrance, I had brought something special for some of the boys, and, when I announced my arrival at the dugout, Goose asked a security guard to take me into the bowels of the stadium and down to the clubhouse. You'll have to figure out the "something special" on your own. I don't have to say shit. Statute of limitations, and whatnot.

Goose was waiting for me in the hallway when I approached the clubhouse entrance. Seated at the door, as kind of doorman/official greeter, was Yogi Berra, whose face was on so many of those baseball cards I ruined in rubber-band wars. At that time, Yogi was still known for fracturing language and keeping a, shall we say, humble profile. It was much later that we discovered he was the richest ex-Yankee of them all. I shouldn't have giggled, when we were introduced. I should have hit him up for a loan.

When we turned the corner into the clubhouse, I walked straight onto Glory Road. Every member of the team hollered "Cleve!" as I entered the room. Eat your heart out, Norm. All you ever had was a bunch of drunks hollering your name. I had the fucking New York Yankees hollering mine. Okay, a few of them were drunks, but still . . . I was greeted as if I were the Sultan of Swat himself.

For that one moment, I was the King of the Hill, the Top of the Mark, the Grand Wazoo, an even hotter Arthur Brown. And I stuck around only long enough to bask without burning. I told Tommy John to win one for me, as he left for his warm-ups, and I left the premises. He pitched a three-hitter. And won. It was the cherry on top of a banana-split entrance. A very tasty sundae, indeed. Nothing so-so-'un about it.

Whatever happened to that revolution we were going to have?

According to history weasels, it disappeared sometime in the late Sixties, right around the time the Haight was declared dead. I disagree. I think the revolution morphed, much like the vaunted revolutionaries who threw down the gauntlet. The path to radical change was itself radicalized. Revolution became a song, then a Broadway play, and a new makeup from Revlon. In 2020, Fiat will introduce its newest model, the Gauntlet 350.

Everybody has a different view of what revolution is or isn't. The first great idea of revolution in my lifetime was the Human Be-In in New York. Revolution through . . . nothing. Five hundred thousand fucking people gathered in Central Park, with absolutely no agenda. The invitation to attend blazed through the hip community. It said, "Come to Central Park and be." Nobody really knew what it meant to just "be," but we all understood we had to be "be" there, with everyone else being . . . be.

Totally revolutionary.

Of course, Stephen and I were mostly there to see if we could cadge a joint or maybe join in on one, that being our goal every day, twenty-four seven. We knew who we wanted to be. More importantly, we knew how we wanted to be: wasted. And there was plenty of dope to be smoked at the Be-In. NYPD, for the first time ever perhaps, couldn't bust us. Too many of us, too few of them. We learned that to win this type of revolution, we'd have to get, like, a hundred-fifty million of us to spliff up and . . . be. You're really looking at the long game here.

I stumbled into a much scarier vision of radical change at just about this same time, when a kinda sorta friend took me over to the East Village to meet some friends of his. He told me they were Weathermen, which I took to mean they were people into climate control. Which meant they were into farming and shit. Farming shit like pot. You can see how my brain works. I was looking for a bud.

In a darkened apartment in the middle of a sunny day, everything and everyone in the room looked gray, and the mood was very serious. My friend introduced me around, including to the leader of the discussion, a guy named Jerry Rubin. Jerry was a short guy, but he was the most energetic person in the room—a room, I might add, that had no marijuana in it. Everyone, including Rubin, spoke in whispers, in case whoever-the-fuck was listening in, and it was all terrifying shit about civil disobedience, bombs, and robbing banks to get the money to finance more mayhem. Jerry gave almost textbook advice on how to do all of the above. What I needed was textbook advice on rolling a fucking joint.

This was not the revolutionary I wanted to be. I bolted

and never looked back at that apartment or the Weathermen. Surely there was a gentler way to topple the government, return power to the masses, and set the chickens free. Perhaps it was to be a combination of these two concepts: get everybody in the country totally baked, *then* blow up stuff.

Then we could all look at each other, holler "cool," and look for more stuff to explode.

I didn't run into Rubin again until I was at the Lone Star Cafe years later. Jerry had moved from storming the Bastille to making a killing on Wall Street. Revolution had devolved, as had Jerry. He no longer wanted to battle the establishment; he wanted to own it. I guess there is some value in this, if you use that ownership to achieve radical change in society. The only radical change Jerry achieved was that he made a butt load of money. He did better than Abbie Hoffman, though, at least financially. By the time Abbie surfaced from his long lam, his new main goal was to be a stand-up comedian. Okay now, that is revolting.

I managed to stumble into active revolution once. I think that's how many people become involved in such things. You know: We just wanted a fair price for tea. We really had no idea England would be so pissy about it and start blowing up stuff without us. If we'd all sat down with our Native American brothers and toked a bit of their private reserve, we could have enjoyed the fireworks together. They blow up one of ours, we blow up one of theirs, we all shake hands and set a good price for English Breakfast. King George would have none of it. He obviously never tried the private reserve.

I had heard about a rally over in Berkeley. I do not remember exactly why it attracted my attention. It involved hippies.

There would be pot. 'Nough said. When I got to the rally at a place called Sproul Plaza, there was already a good deal of tension in the air. No cutesy moments of hippie girls sticking flowers in police gun barrels. The gun barrels were there, and the cops sporting them looked more than a little grumpy. They had established what I would later learn was called a perimeter—around what, I could not see. I saw no flowers anywhere. And no pot. Fuck me. What had I walked into?

A sideways glimpse of a brick flying toward the perimeter from behind me fairly informed me. I was three blocks away by the time that brick landed, and back in the Haight in less than forty minutes. I don't even remember how I got home—bus, hitchhike? I could have run the distance no problem, I was so shaken. I later learned the whole place went bazooka right after that brick hit, and one guy was even killed. It became known as the Peace Park Riot, Bloody Thursday. Or, as I like to call it, There Was No Pot, And I Shit My Pants Day.

Lesson learned, to be sure, so when a riot broke out on Haight Street soon after this one, I stayed in the house at 408 Cole St. and watched the action from the bay window with the rest of the delinquents. Delinquent, yes, but not stupid enough to engage in Molotov cocktail shit. And cocktails were flying on Haight Street, two blocks away. After the first one popped and lit up the storefront behind it like a klieg light, someone on the block between us and the action started playing Dylan's "Masters of War" out his window, full volume. And *voilà!* It's Andrew Lloyd Webber's fab new musical, *Hello Molotov!*

Right. The whole feel of the Haight Street episode was more street theater than revolution. The unfortunate reality of revolution is that someone gets killed, probably a bunch of someones. This was not that. The Haight Street Riot had real urgency, but it also showed the difference between Berkeley and the Haight. Berkeley was politically radical. The Haight was chemically radical. Every one of the cocktail-tossers in the Haight would rather have been home smoking a fatty. Like the family in the bay window at 408 Cole St.

The two events convinced me that you've really got to stay focused if you are going to revolt and overthrow with violence. And you have to remain focused for a fuck of a long time. You will have to give up smoking dope altogether. *Shudder.*

The best kind of revolution I have ever seen was practiced by the late, and dearly missed, Bobby Lee, the former Chicago Black Panther and a cousin of Panther founder Bobby Seale. I met Bobby late in his life, when he was a frail old man in a wheelchair. He may have been physically frail, but he was a dynamo in spirit who never stopped helping, organizing, and leading his community until the last day of his life. Bobby didn't just practice revolution; he *was* revolution. More importantly, he loved smoking high-grade weed. Now that's an achiever.

As a young Panther, Bobby was the co-founder of the original Rainbow Coalition. He always said the coalition was the establishment's worst nightmare, and he was right. It was a type of revolution that could work. Luckily for all of us, the coalition was merely the blueprint for how he lived the rest of his life—organizing communities, advising campaigns, and championing causes. Politicos and powerbrokers still hate that shit. They would go Section 8 Flight Deck if there were, like, eight or ten million Bobby Lees.

Their problem is they can't shoot you for being a great guy, or for making sure a community's children are being fed breakfast, or for stopping by all the older folks' homes to make sure they have blankets. At least not as of 10 p.m. this evening.

Maybe revolution has changed. I know I have. I still believe it may be necessary. Our universe is filled with so much dark matter, it may take something extraordinary to bring forth the light. When the revolution does start, I will be there. I'll be serving cookies and rolling joints behind the lines.

So . . . I am 230281

No, this is not some sort of West Virginia RFD six-digit phone number, nor is it a numerological description of my character. Yes, it could be my IQ, if you believe my enormous ego, but it it's not that either. It's my prison ID number, provided by my dear friends at the TDC (Texas Department of Corrections). It was lovingly bestowed upon me on my arrival in Huntsville, Texas, in 1973, given in a trade for my waist-length hair and dignity. I'm sure some crimson-necked troll out there will cheer that this was a fair trade, that the hippie boy deserved life, rather than the seven-year sentence the hippie boy received. Let me just speak to those jive-ass dickwads first: Fuck you, trolls.

It was the worst trade of my life, but I did kind of ask for it. I was the one caught nearly three years earlier on a commercial flight bound for the Big Apple with fifteen pounds of high-grade pot, busted by no less than the captain of the Austin vice squad, Harvey Gann. I was the careless criminal, the one who inevitably gets caught, the one who should never have chosen that line of work in the first place. You may now rest the thought that my IQ is anywhere near 230281.

My attorney, he with the acme of Texas names, Sam Houston Clinton Jr., had done his legal-beagle best to keep me out of the cell block—he ran it all the way up to the Supreme Court. But I finally had to say my goodbyes, turn myself in, get my new number, and plan my suicide. I did not find out until recently that the focus of my appeal was not that the Braniff employees opened my bag illegally. It was on the notion that pot shouldn't have been illegal in the first place. Which makes my overall view of his representation somewhat ambivalent. He didn't keep me out of the slam, but he was a totally righteous dude. Totally.

And he turned out to be one of those mystery pieces in the jigsaw puzzle I call my life. The two-and-a-half years of appeals kept me out on bail and gave me a few extra universal minutes to figure out what piece of that puzzle came next. Pot dealing had been my first (and really only) career choice, and it was a had-to situation. I had begat my first-born, Harmony, with Little Nancy, so I had to figure out how to not be the good-for-nothing mooch I was born to be. I had to get a job, but with zero experience with anything. Literally anything. My stay in the ad world had been too short to learn dick, and my brief stint as a shill in the Village offered few opportunities in Austin. There were no three-card monte players here, so far as I knew. I had survived a gig at the post office in San Francisco, but I learned only two skills there—how to sort shit alphabetically, and how to stack mail sacks in a way that left a little sleeping den at the bottom. We shit-sorters were always tired bears.

Well into my sixth year of no haircuts, I saw only two paths ahead of me. I could either take a dishwasher job being offered at the Bag End restaurant, a job that could lead to a career as . . . a waiter. Or I could be a rock star. Again, please hark back to my IQ numbers, when I tell you I initially opted for the former—for about two weeks, before the realization that at the age of twenty-six, I was already a blossoming curmudgeon, and potentially the first waiter to go postal. And the grease. What can I say about the grease? It was my ever-present companion. Gotta love the grease, if you take path number one.

Before I threw in the brush, rag, and apron, though, I asked Bo, the owner of the joint, if I could put a chair in the middle of the dining room and play some songs—nine to be exact. I did this a couple times, but my rhythm section of knives, forks, and glasses was just not up to snuff. The center of a vegetarian restaurant, sans PA system, was not the stage of my dreams either. I did learn a thing or two about playing to a dinner theater crowd, which I've never again had to do in my entire fucking life.

Fortunately, Big Rikke, aka the Guacamole Queen, had other plans for me. She always did. To be frank, I'm shocked we don't have an annual Guacamole Queen Day in Austin in her honor. And still amazed at all she did for the entire armadillo universe. Anyway, she was the cook at the Bag End at that time and had seen my "act." She went all out and got me an opening slot at the One Knite. The One Knite was special cool, the real down-low in Austin clubs, the perfect joint for my growl of an act. I was ecstatic. I had but one question: What was an opening slot?

I was doing an opening set for Storm with Jimmie Vaughan and Doyle Bramhall Sr. I quickly learned the meaning of "opening slot": It meant eat-shit comeuppance. I played my ten songs (yeah, I went all out and added a new song), repeated a couple when the set was too short, and fell apart the minute these guys started playing. Doyle had one of the richest, most perfect blues voices I'd ever heard, and Jimmie was already a seasoned stylist who could fool you into thinking he wasn't on it at the starts to songs, only to blister you with searing this-hurts-so-much-from-the-inside solos. I was fucking Howdy Doody.

I wanted a band, like Jimmie and Doyle. Fuck that, I wanted to be Jimmie and Doyle. And of course Big Rikke had a plan. Always a plan with the queen. She told me to go see a guy named Mike on Oakland Street. That was another thing about Big Rikke. She didn't ask you to do shit, she told you to do shit. You did shit. You did not give her shit back.

Mike was (the now late) Mike Pugh, who played bass, had an amp, and didn't hate me right off the bat. Many folks have. I wear that as a badge. To my surprise and instant delight, Mike had invited Pat Pankratz, a really fluid, melodic, and instinctive guitar player, to join us. Suddenly all my songs sounded really fucking good. Mike's instincts were ever as good as Pat's, and Pat's voice was a million times better than mine. Both were schooled enough to cover my raw, barely adequate skills and were, even more amazingly, willing to let me be leader of the band.

Which meant, we were a band. Just like that. All we needed was a name. I'm not sure if my recent experiences sliding across the floor of the Bag End had anything to do with it, but I proposed the name Greezy Wheels. It was the coolest nickname I'd ever acquired as a kid—lots better than Clem, my second-best childhood nickname, therefore the worst childhood nickname. The boys went for it, with an addendum. We were all into Mungo Jerry and the idea of skiffle bands, and we already could feel that kind of oeuvre developing. We went with the Greezy Wheels Skiffle Band. And it took us places (with a slight name change) almost immediately. Greezy Wheels is one of my proudest achievements to this day. That and my amazing eggplant parmesan.

And that was the Sam Houston puzzle piece. By giving me time with appeals, he had also given me something I'd never had before: purpose and focus. Oh yeah, and a whole lot more than that. Yepper, a whole lot more.

Now, where the fuck was I?

Two and a half years later, I was driven down to Huntsville in chains. Never one with a strong bladder, I had to urinate about every thirty minutes. The sheriff driving us only stopped once from Austin to Huntsville. That's two hours and forty minutes. Do the math. Feel the pain.

I'd hoped to pay for a haircut at the county jail when I turned myself in, but they sent us down the following morning. I was the belle of the ball the minute I stepped out of the car at Diagnostics, the place where they decide which unit will be your home. We were led into a dank reception area, where we were told to strip, bend over, and spread 'em—adios dignity—before they blasted us with flea powder. I got a taste of it as it hit my lips. It displayed a delightful piquancy.

Then went the hair, a good two feet of prime, thick, healthy young male hair. They clipped it shave-close to my head so they could sell it to a wig maker. I thought about asking them for a cut on the sale, but kept lips zipped. Lurid comments about my "pussy fine" asshole were lingering in the air, and I was still starkos.

Finally they handed us some clothes—white shirt, pants, and undies, black shoes and socks. Perfect: my spring colors. Our clothes were tagged with our numbers. The guy in front of me was 230280, and I was 230281. Good thing. I could never have been 230280.

Watching stars birth is what it's all about

When you spend fifty years in music, watching, playing and promoting acts old and new, you are bound to get an occasional view of genius at its very blossoming. You just happen to be there when somebody blows the world away or is just about to. You consider yourself a very lucky person. Theoretically anyway. Unfortunately the speed of life doesn't always allow you to appreciate exactly what you've seen and heard. Until you're fucking seventy years old.

I have been very surprised to discover that I do still own all these memories, sometimes in great detail, sometimes a bit vaguely. I recall vividly, for example, Led Zeppelin's first ever shows at the Fillmore East. The first footage is of them exploding onto the stage—they literally ran out, Jimmy's guitar already ablaze, band already on fire—for each of the eight performances they gave that week. The next memory is of the entire second balcony, which I was working, running to the front rail every time they hit. I was absolutely sure a major lemming incident was imminent. Or possibly the collapse of the front of the balcony. I voted for the former, figuring I could survive the fall of the lemmings by simply not joining them. Stupid lemmings . . .

The wrap of that memory was of the poor bastards headlining over them and being killed, show after show, night after night: Iron Butterfly, whose guitarist could not match Page in any way except natty attire. There was no question that Zep had arrived and was gonna be here for a while. I've never been a giant Plant fan, but—and maybe this was the lighting—he sparkled. Like stardust. You just had to love his smart-ass cockiness, the way he swung a mic around, and the bulge in his skin tights. Yeah, he was a star. The pants said so.

Sometimes I've merely crossed paths with that "next big thing." Mary and I occasionally took a car service into work at the Lone Star from our Brooklyn Heights hermitage, every now and then sharing with other riders for convenience. On one particular evening a young woman was seated in the front seat when we entered the car. Within the first minutes of our ride in, she turned to us and said: "My name is Juice. You're going to be hearing about me."

Of course it was Juice Newton, and she hit the charts less than two months later. Makes me wonder: Is smart-ass cockiness the key to stardom? If so, why am I not swimming in gold, like Scrooge fucking McDuck?

I didn't always see exactly what it was everyone was talking about. It was easy to see George Strait was on his way when he played the Lone Star for a live WHN radio broadcast. I became even more aware of his impending superstardom when he told me that he was a fan of the Greezy Wheels, that he used to come see us at the Cheatham Street Warehouse. I guess I'm that way: If they like me, I see them.

But I didn't really get it with Reba McEntire when she came in for her WHN broadcast. She was a real sweetheart, for sure, and her show was ultra pro, but I admit that I do have a harder time finding the genius in late-century Nashville music. The only sparkle I saw in Reba was in the slight dizziness I felt trying to talk to her ever-so-slightly crossed eyes.

It's hard to look into a person's inner being when one eye is a left turn.

If at first you don't succeed, try to see it again. My first Velvet Underground show was rock-and-roll with a fright wig, every bit as bizarre as the venue in which they played, the Balloon Farm. The Farm was Warhol's first experiment in performance art. It appeared one summer on the second floor of a building on St. Mark's Place in the East Village, the one-time center of hippie culture and home to the infamous street band of revolutionaries, David Peel and the Lower East Side. You might remember that John Lennon actually sat in with these folks. Not for long, though—David was a bit too outré even for John.

The Balloon Farm was just a big ole gym-like hall with a stage at one end. The first "show" I had attended there had been a two-thousand-person jam session. Andy had invited one and all to come to the Farm and bring an instrument. Big mistake. I did not see much genius in a hundred and twenty decibels of un-music. And I didn't see a whole lot of brilliance at that first Underground show, either. For some ungodly reason, Sterling Morrison decided to play his guitar at sonic-boom level with a violin bow . . . on every single tune. It was a wall of ouch. I'm pretty sure the minor tinnitus I experience today came from that caterwaul.

Luckily, I did see them again, and more luckily, it was brilliant. I caught them at the Vulcan Gas Company in Austin, another big ole gym-like hall, but this time Lou Reed was in firm control of the band. It was all there—the rough-trade lyrics, the incessantness of the moment, the curl of Reed's lip. That is star stuff, folks. I never looked at his pants to see if it was Robert Plant star stuff, but one could not ignore the obvious. Lou was the deal.

By far, the greatest joy I ever got watching the rise of a big-timer came from our own Stevie Ray. By the time Mary and I migrated to NYC, Austin knew all about the kid with the magic fingers and incredible tone. I had first caught him at a Cobras gig in Northwest Park. I hadn't seen Paul Ray and the boys for a while, and when I got out of the car, I was transfixed by a guitar coming from another dimension. Okay, it was the same dimension, just on the other side of the hill. But it was dimensional, in a way.

It harkened me back to my first days in Austin in 1969, when I kept hearing this amazing guitarist rehearsing around the corner. Every day I would be astonished anew by this guy, who turned out to be the late Jesse Taylor, one of the very best slingers Texas (specifically Lubbock) has ever produced. Yeah, he was that good. And he could also kick the shit out of you if you pissed him off. Which, in my case, was never.

But there was something else going on with the guitar on the other side of the hill. It had a fluidity that even the greatest players only achieve in spurts. This guitar had unstoppable flow. With no mistakes. At all. Trust me, guitar players watching other guitar players know when a lick is missed. In most cases, great guitarists deliver great recoveries, but for that one brief second, the player's pants are on the floor. He is exposed. And the other guitar player knows it. Stevie's pants never hit the floor.

A couple years later, Stevie was touring the east with Triple Threat, featuring Lou Ann Barton and including our ex-Greezy Wheels drummer, Chris Layton. I fat-armed Mort into booking him into the Lone Star for the princely sum of a hundred bucks. I cannot recall who headlined that show, and I'll wager no one else who was there remembers, either. This was Stevie's first shot at a New York audience, and for those few who saw it, it was the shot heard 'round the world.

Unfortunately for LouLou—not so much. Lou Ann began knocking back shots in double time and, during the break between shows, started throwing glasses at the waitresses. We had no choice but to send her back to the hotel. For the second set, Stevie would sing all the songs, and I do believe that was the very first time he did so. It was a revelation. He had a perfect voice for rhythm-and-blues, and I think he challenged himself to play even better to obscure any insecurities he might have had.

And obscure, he did. To this day, I am convinced he blistered the paint behind the bar. It hadn't looked sweated out like that before this show. It did ever after. At the end of his set, he sat down on the edge of the stage and tore the universe a new asshole over the final five minutes. By the time he finished, nearly everybody there had gathered up close to him, wanting to see if they could capture just a taste of whatever the fuck was driving this skinny little guy from Texas.

And Mort was there to see it all. He witnessed every harrowing moment on the edge, every brilliant stroke. There was absolutely no mistaking that this star was fully birthed. Surely he had seen it too. I was dying to know what he thought. Mort's response? "Too loud." Maybe Mort didn't get a good look at Stevie's pants.

I am two degrees of holy shit

By now, we've all figured out that pretty much everyone on the planet is within six degrees of Kevin Bacon, Walt Disney, and John Wayne Gacy. Two degrees bring shit a little closer to home. It's true I have been lucky enough to be one degree from all kinds of cool people, and I do love to prattle on about that. That I know people is a major portion of my personality. Yes, I'm that shallow. But I probably take my greatest pride in being two degrees of holy shit.

It's almost astonishing to me that in all the years I have matriculated through the netherworld of the music business, I have never met Bob Dylan face to face. I am within two degrees of him in so many ways I have lost count. And as large a shadow as he casts, I don't think of him as holy shit, anyway. Good shit, yes. Maybe even great shit, though I should insert here that I rarely use the term "great shit" in regard to anything other than the highest-grade pot.

I'm one degree to nearly all of Bob's band members over the last half century: His manager used to be an annoying newbie agent I knew at ICM, and I once knew a guy named Tony, an intellectually challenged person, who did odd jobs in the Village in the Sixties and looked exactly like Bob. Even closer to my magic one degree of Bob is Kinky. Big Dick and Zimmerman have been friends for decades. Bob once asked Kinky to write an album together. Kinky demurred. I should mention here that Kinky likes to pee himself every so often.

Kinky did get me close one night, when we stood in reception-line formation backstage at an Austin show twenty or so years ago, expecting to say hello to Bob as he took the stage. The curse of one degree struck, when Bob entered the stage from the opposite side. Malicious intent? Bob absolutely knew that Kinky (and Doug Sahm) were waiting there to see him. Maybe Bob has a reception-line phobia. Or maybe he's just a dick. Regardless, it pissed Kinky off. Really, really pissed him off. Kinky does hate reception lines, bitched the entire time we waited in it, and went berserkers when the music started and Bob began to sing. Which made for a terrific night for me. Schadenfreude and me—we tight.

Halfway through Bob's set, my evening was made. As Kinky and I watched with Bobbie Nelson from the wings, he grew ever more churlish. By mid-set he was seething. When Bob finished yet another of the many songs that sounded nothing like the original versions, Kinky yelled, "When the fuck is he going to play 'All Along the Watchtower?'"

To which Bobbie replied, "Kinky, honey, he just did."

I believe Kinky came as close to stroking out as one can come without losing consciousness. I bugged out right after that. It's always good to leave on a high note.

My real brush with ultimate degrees of holy shit occurred nearly thirty years before this, with the very first band I saw at the Night Owl in the Village. My first show was a three-band bill of the Fugitives, the Strangers, and the Magicians. The first one to play was the Fugitives, a kinda sorta Beatle-looking quartet. I liked them enough to mention them to the talent buyer at J. Walter Thompson, which got them some work and some referrals. It got me access into their world: I was allowed to hang out with them. Please, folks, do not do this at home. You do not want to give me access.

I mostly hung with the Fugitives' co-leaders, Phil and Evan, both of whom sang and wrote. Phil Feliciotto, who had a killer tenor, was the one most dedicated to the actual making and performing of music. You knew it was his life the minute he stepped on stage. His set-closer version of "Somewhere Over the Rainbow" even impressed me, and I fucking hate the song. He would later change his name to Phil Cody and co-write big hits with Neil Sedaka in the Seventies. Good tunes with good dance beats. Dick Clark Dance Party specials, but not holy shit.

Evan Charmatz was a whole other ball of confusion. Though he took his music seriously, what he was really looking for was The Life. His parents had programmed him and his brother Ray to be a dentist and a lawyer, respectively, from the day they were born. The Village, the Fugitives, and the music were their daring escape from Not The Life. Just like a good ninety percent of every other band that has ever taken the stage. Evan, though, had a special path to take in his life—the one that got me to two degrees of holy shit. Evan was nearly holy shit all by himself.

I spent many all-nighters hanging with Evan and his pal, Danny Plumer, at the historically funky Albert Hotel at the corner of Tenth Street and University Place. The Albert was a half-step above fleabag, mostly because it had an actual bellhop, Hallie, who was mid-seventies when we met him. Real fleabags don't have bellhops. They have fleas. Unfortunately, neither Hallie nor the fleas carried your bags.

The Albert was a musician favorite: For price and location, it could not be beat, but the fact that nobody gave two shits about the constant pot-smoke haze in the hallways established it as a tour destination. Both the Lovin' Spoonful and the Mothers rehearsed in the basement, and it was the scene of the first major hotel-room trashing by a band, the Blues Magoos. You heard it here: The Magoos predated Keith Moon.

The hotel was built around an air shaft, and one evening, Pepi, the Magoos' guitarist/singer/spark plug accidentally knocked a beer bottle off the sill into the shaft. When the bottle hit the ground ten floors later, the explosion was so loud it rattled the windows. Pepi simply had to do it again, and again and again and again, until everything in the room that could fit through the window—side tables, chairs, whatever—went through the window. You had to hand it to the Magoos. They had also just figured out how to trash a room without making a mess. The total cost for damages was probably less than a hundred bucks.

Rooms at the Albert cost ten bucks, so it was easy to put together enough to rent one. Over a period of a summer, we probably did it four or five times, whenever we had a couple joints or whatever designer drug was on the menu that week. Evan's girlfriend, Mona, was a nurse, so we always got first choice of appetizers.

Most of our evenings at the Albert with Danny and Evan (and sometimes Evan's brother, Ray, the drummer) were about Evan. Danny was kind of an outlier stylistically, who didn't look or dress hippie *or* Carnaby. In fact, he had a kind of young Sinatra thing going on. But he knew how to talk to his good friend, Evan, who really wanted to be John Lennon. These late nights and all-nighters were shrink sessions of the highest degree, depending of course on how high we managed to get.

Evan would decry the fate that awaited him in Not The Life, and Danny would do his best to keep Evan focused on The Life—until Danny got as wasted as Evan and everything devolved into a soppy mess. I was usually at soppy mess long before them, therefore too stoned to speak. Can you imagine—me, unable to speak? Evan even nicknamed me "The Owl" because of my saucer (read: wasted) eyes and eerie quiet (read: super wasted). But Owl was learning stuff, like maybe Evan was a little messed up. Or maybe Owl was a little messed up.

One way or t'other, I drifted away from the Fugitives, and life went on. Forty years later, I discovered my two degrees of holy shit through Evan. Evan became . . . a dentist, but not just any dentist: the dentist to the stars, with a luxe office in Hollywood. He changed his last name to Chandler (as did his brother, who became . . . Raymond Chandler) and may have actually found The Life. He kept recording his songs, met everyone there was to meet in LaLa, and even co-wrote the movie "Robin Hood: Men In Tights" with Mel Brooks. Which brings us right up to the shit that is holy.

It turns out it was Evan's son to whom Michael Jackson had to pay twenty million bucks to keep his lips zipped over whatever Michael's lips had done. Holy shit.

Jazz musicians are just rock musicians with more chords

If I thought I was entering a more bucolic world when I moved from the nightly honky-tonk madness of the Lone Star Cafe to the elegant world of the Blue Note Jazz Club, I was mistaken. The Blue Note may represent the epitome of bucolic, but the people who work and play the joint are anything but. Who do you think taught rock musicians how to get fucked up? It was all those fucked-up jazzers who predated us.

All club gigs are the same in one respect. They demand an unreasonable amount of your valuable time. When I refer to my valuable time, I'm of course talking about down time, the moments when I can lie in virtual state, drawing imaginary little circles around my belly button. That's right—you heard it—I'm a sloth. Inherently, nightclub management may not have been my best choice.

Whereas the music at the Lone Star generally finished up before 2 a.m. most nights, the jam session at the Blue Note *started* at 2 a.m. every night. The evening feature may have been a cool breeze, like MJQ or Stanley Turrentine, but we had to start shit all over at two, with the great, and severely unsung, Ted Curson hosting the jam session. Not that it mattered that Ted was terrific. The regulars who showed up each night remain unsung for a good reason. If we weren't tired after the main act, we were sleepwalking midway through the jam.

But at the same time, you had to stay on your toes. You never knew when the humdrum of standards being played badly would be displaced for one magical instant by an amazing one-of-a-kind, never-to-be-repeated performance. Perhaps the greatest of these was the night Al Jarreau, Nancy Wilson, George Benson, and Bobby McFerrin took the stage together and had a scat-off. For a solid ten minutes, four of the world's greatest interpreters of scat one-upped each other, bringing the entire audience to its feet. The entire audience of ten.

When they finished, they all left together to party into the night. Which was what I hadn't figured into the equation: Almost everyone who played the Blue Note partied on into the night after the shows. They went to all-night jam sessions, all-night bars, all-night parties, all-night whatever. Just like fucking Keith Moon.

Many of the old-school cool, like Herbie Mann, who always had the best pot, or Milt Jackson, who moved the way he played the vibes, gliding over the notes, came and went smooth. But there were some who flew into the place on jet packs, stayed cranked until week's end (all the headliners did six days), and left us in a state of exhaustion. Believe it or not, Sarah Vaughan was one of those. Sassy Sarah was nearly sixty, but every minute of her life was still a hard charge. Like a taser. She nearly killed me.

On the first night of what was a very special week for us,

Sarah kept me, her band, and a couple who-the-fuck-was-thats up and at 'em all night in my office on the second floor. Every time I'd make a noise about bugging out, Sarah would say, "Let's do another blast, hon."

How could I refuse a life-long idol . . . or the offer to do another blast? Bad etiquette either way.

Sarah also practically chain-smoked cigarettes—astonishing, considering how amazing her voice still was. I'm pretty sure everyone else in my office was smoking as well. By the time we opened the shutter windows overlooking Third Street from the second floor, a cloud of smoke puffed out into the mid-morning gloom. Somehow mornings are always a bit gloomy when you encounter them after blowing shit up your nose all night. I don't think Sarah saw it that way.

She was completely unaffected. I had a headache for the rest of the week. Felt like shit (sometimes proper etiquette will do that to you). Sarah bounced in the next night, slapped me on the fanny, and said, "Let's get to work, sweetie."

And there she went. She rocked the joint five straight nights at full-on Sass. I managed to avoid further chemical aftermath by begging off. Yes, I am just a big old pussy next to Sassy Sarah. Big old pussy rock musician.

I'm not even that next to Jaco Pastorius. Sarah may have partied all night, but she at least went to bed and slept late. Jaco didn't sleep. By the time I met him, he was doing mountains of blow and exploring the musical sounds of the asteroid belt. He needed rocket fuel by the ounce for the mission, and he asked me to help him gas up. I couldn't get him the amounts he needed—nor did I want to—but I could get him work. What part of the solar system he intended to explore next was none of my business. I convinced Schlomo, my boss, to book him for at least three full weeks over the next months, and I got Mort at the Lone Star to pick up several more one-offs.

Schlomo was quite pleased when Jaco's first week came close to selling out every night. What Schlomo didn't see was how that week progressed. Jaco literally did not sleep for the rest of the week. Each day brought an ever more disengaged Jaco. Each day also brought another level of performance, and contrary to what you might think, the levels were rising, not sinking. Jaco had put together one mother of a band, led by Hiram Bullock, and no matter how high or far out he asked them to go with him, the band nailed it. Fuck—they built that city. By Saturday night, there was a genuine fear the stage might self-combust.

I feared for that lad. A lot. He was such a sweetheart at his core, but he was such a mess everywhere else. I knew better than to hang too close—call it the Vaughan Experience—so there wasn't much more I could do to stop what turned out to be a fully formed spiral down. The last time I saw Jaco was when he showed up at a Carmen McRae show, asking me to let him in to talk to Ray Brown. Normally, no problem. But not when you are barefoot, shirtless, with black smudges under your eyes, pro football style. The audience was black tie, not black smudge.

It broke my heart to deny him entrance, but I had to. To protect him. From himself. I feared for that lad, because I loved that lad. I have no idea if getting closer to him than I actually did would have helped him. I don't think it would have helped me much. Turns out it's good to be a big ole pussy rock musician. I've learned at least four or five new chords in my old age.

The best way to get through a prison sentence is to get a good nickname

You can't really give yourself one, and you don't want most of the nicknames available. Mostly, you just have to be lucky enough to not be killed or molested by weightlifter guys named "Big Judy" or Mexican Mafia members named "Mi Casa, Su Casa" (more a summons than an invitation—trust me). If you survive long enough without being named "Lola," you will earn an acceptable nickname. You will earn your nickname by your method of survival.

Once a new convict is sorted, tested, and graded at Diagnostics in the Texas prison system, he is sent to one of many units scattered around the state. There are probably, like, a hundred of these units now, but when I was the new stud on campus, there were maybe seven or eight. Of these, there were a couple—Eastham and Ellis—that you did everything in your power to avoid. Judy and Mi Casa were there waiting for you, and you'd likely spend your entire sentence working days in cotton rows and nights in *flagrante delicto*.

As that was not my chosen profession, nor my chosen flagrante, I did everything I could at Diagnostics to be sent to the "Walls," the original Huntsville prison, once inhabited by John Wesley Harding. I knew there'd be some negotiating there, but it wasn't a farm, therefore no opportunity for others to notice my gorgeous butt while I'm bent over picking cotton. I already knew the drill in the showers—pick your spots, don't sing, don't ever pick up the fucking soap.

I did manage to get assigned to the Walls after working in the Diagnostic cafeteria shucking shit, snapping shit, chopping shit, and avoiding most of the shit I saw coming through the back door. It was a TDC tradition that the guards stole all the good cuts of meat, and we were served hot dogs that had a lethal red-dye look to them with spots of blue. I lost weight, but I got good reports from the guards. When three others and I were bused through the back gates of the Walls and deposited in the factory area—bound for the Major's office (the major being the head cop) for formal introductions—we learned the first nickname absolutely everyone acquires as he arrives at his new home. He is a "drive-up." Right: That means we just drove up. A short-term nickname, disposable as it were. No worries. You're only a drive-up once. Ever after, you are just another schmuck convict.

The second nickname was one available to any of the four of us as we passed through the tunnel into the prison yard. This was "My Kid," which was what the older convicts sitting along the brick wall were hoping to call any one of us. To be someone's kid quite simply meant you were his girlfriend. Again, not my preferred flagrante. Lucky for me, I wasn't anybody's focus. I'd slipped past svelte into concentration-camp chic when I hit 165 pounds at Diagnostic. You could tell I had good bones, because you could fucking see them. Which only enhanced my chinless-ness. I was not a catch. For any sex. Or species.

I was a guy with ideas, though. After spending a month working in a hundred twenty decibels of machine noise and a permanent fog of cotton dust at the Walls cotton gin, I was reassigned to the hospital, where a whole lot of other guys with ideas worked. I immediately became pals with the late Buck Lovett, who had the biggest ideas. He had figured out how to smuggle pot into the Walls, using trustees training to be telephone linemen on a nearby Texas A&M campus. You can see why Buck and I hit it off.

As soon as I told him and our fellow conspirators that my Greezy Wheels bandmates could supply the pot, I became "Greezy." The name became nearly legendary, at least within the confines, when the band delivered the goods. Oh yeah, I was cool. Though I only got a few skinny joints out of it, every convict in the unit got a buzz. A couple guys even got busted in another cellblock, having forgotten to mix it with Prince Albert tobacco, the most god-awful stinky tobacco ever grown—therefore free to felons.

I became a protected species, one that would definitely not go extinct anywhere in the vicinity. I was given back-bench TV privileges by Big Judy and Mi Casa, Su Casa without having to be friends with benefits. I could choose a show, and nobody in the front benches could fuck with me. We could watch shit like "Don Kirshner's Rock Concert" instead of "One Day at a Time." My viewing choices received mixed responses. "One Day at a Time" was big with the I-once-killed-a-redhead set.

I got a new cellmate, Leroy Moore, the hospital cook, so I could finally eat decent food, and I became pals with a number of the brothers who played b-ball on lunch break. Hanging with the brothers was something few of the guys in my tank did. But for me, this was where it got good. I didn't just have the one nickname. I was so fucking cool, I got two more. Neither involved kids.

I was a pretty good baller in my youth. No vertical leap—I believe I once jumped over a telephone book—but a sweet jump shot from just about anywhere, especially the corner. And I'd play with anybody, any size, any time. I wasn't fearless, merely a little slow to accept my limitations (read: phone-book leap). I became the "Grey Ghost" when one of the ballers first saw me walk on the court in the afternoon sun. My normal skin color is a fine grey porcelain. Fuck it, I'm nearly transparent. Good nickname. But he picked me for his team, and we became friends. It was a kind of an ebony-and-ivory thing. Without the singing.

The real stud-ness attached itself to me with my corner shot. I became a first or second pick for teams every day. Maybe two weeks after introducing myself to the ball court, the same guy who named me Grey Ghost introduced me to a drive-up as "Jerry West." My full rep was made. I was later the only white boy on the unit basketball team. I never got any rebounds, and I wasn't the guy you wanted bringing the ball up court. Hell, I rarely ran the length of the court, but when we needed clutch, Jerry West was there.

The Major was always looking for something on me,

but he could never pin anything on my adorable ass, including whether or not the drawings my children sent me had LSD on them. They didn't—we could get acid elsewhere—but I loved that it drove him nuts. He knew about the nicknames. He also knew that if you had one, you were clearly up to something. Oh yes, I was clearly up to something. Big ideas abound in small places.

Not all rock managers are dicks

Just an alarmingly high percentage of them. It comes with the territory. A manager is here to serve the rock star, whether that rock star is aspiring or big time, and it is uncanny how equally difficult both aspiring and big-time stars can be. To serve these little monsters—especially the aspirational—a manager must develop a personality that both clicks his heels at every rock-star whim and snaps a bullwhip at the unfortunate suckers that want to book or record that rock star. He starts shedding skin, becoming more and more lizard-like, with every shedding. He is developing dick.

I do know some great people who have had long and successful careers in the management business—folks I'd hesitate to accuse of being pure dicks—but even they will stab you in the eye in front of your children if you seriously dis one of their acts. In fact, there are levels of dick. And, like fingerprints, a zillion never-two-the-same kinds of dick. Having dealt with about half a zillion managers over the years, I have developed an extremely accurate internal dick-o-meter. I can spot a total hard-on across a stadium.

The meter registered off the charts with Albert Grossman, with whom I experienced several meetings while working the "hole" at the Fillmore East in the later Sixties. The hole was the entrance from the audience to the stage, and rather than coming through the backstage, Albert always insisted on parading down the aisle with a gaggle of young women he would be "happy to introduce" to whichever star was playing that night (and for a while, he managed a lot of them). This guy sashayed dick.

I had early on witnessed how he treated Janis Joplin, one of his clients. That big ole hunk of Ben Franklin-looking harmlessness was a pig. A pig with paws. He was all over her, a real lizard. If the MeToo generation were to catch him today, he'd be roasted. Not on a stage—on a spit. I had a bit of a proprietary thing with Janis: She and I had flirted several times since I first come-hithered her in the Panhandle of Golden Gate Park. Nothing but smiles and lingering eyes, but enough for me to put on my Sir Galahad for her. Or at least represent.

On his third pass through my sentry post, after letting him pass through un-detained his first two times, I stopped him and asked, "And how many people in your coterie this evening, Mr. Grossman?"

Said with a smirk. I have a pretty good smirk, when I need one. My most intense smirk evokes Mr. Sardonicus. Chilling.

I am guessing not many among the living have ever seen Ben Franklin's actual head explode. I did. Apparently I had some fucking nerve for calling his gaggle a coterie. I was also a worthless piece of shit, whose ass was about to be fired. You know, lots of good stuff. I am sure the entire auditorium heard the tirade. It was a beautiful thing. I cherish the memory. I was not fired.

When it comes to high-level dickiness, few people will ever match Jake Riviera in shear kinetic energy. Maybe he was hitting the marching powder, maybe he was just . . . kinetic. I had my first run-in with him on the occasion of a four-clubs-in-an-afternoon tour of New York by Elvis Costello and the Attractions. The Lone Star Cafe was one of those clubs. Jake was Elvis's manager at that time. I loved Elvis, but I'd have much rather gone to see him at CBGB's than produce the event and not see shit. We were slammed within minutes of the announcements going out. Security was skin-tight. Very much like Elvis's pants.

We were told that for this show, we could not open the door to the management offices downstairs to anyone without asking if it was the big bad wolf. It never was, but I follow orders. While I was counting out some cash, a very loud knock interrupted me. When I asked who it was, the reply was, "Open the fucking door!"

Since the accent was whiny cockney punk, I had a hunch it was not the wolf. I opened the door. It was Jake You're-Going-to-Need-a-New-Dick-o-Meter Riviera, and he already hated me. From that second on, he was a total prick.

He had arrived about thirty minutes ahead of the band to make sure everything ran smoothly. Or more succinctly, to make my life miserable. He commandeered my office—he actually tossed me out of it—and started barking orders at me. He needed minute details about the stage set-up that sent me yo-yo-ing up and down the stairs between the office and the stage every three or four minutes until showtime. Not one of these details would make a bit of difference in the performance. When Elvis and the band entered through the back door, I had to tear ass up the stairs again to make sure everything was ready. On the last trip down to tell him it was, Jake pushed me out of the way and led the band past me up the stairs. His ever-so-charming last words to me that day were, "Get the fuck out of the way."

You had to love his consistency. Pure douche.

You must know that in talking about the dick-o-meter, I would have to get around to the slippery dick eventually. The slippery dicks are the cobra-like weasels who slither in, bite you in the ass, and slide out, before you can look at your ass in the mirror. I would have to put Gino McCoslin into this group. This guy was as slippery as they come. He's the guy who, when he booked Willie (Nelson, of course—is there any other Willie?) into a too-small club and the fire marshall applied a one-out-one-in policy, put "Men's Room" and "Women's Room" signs over two exits. When anyone mistakenly walked through either, they were the one-out. Gino knew how to turn a room.

I believe he actually was Willie's manager for a while, having run a club and all kinds of whatever-makes-the-money promotions in Dallas. He definitely was the producer of Willie's picnic at the speedway in College Station. That picnic had to have been the hottest of them all, and there have been some real scorchers. In fact, I'm pretty sure it's in Willie's contract that the temperature must always be a hundred degrees or more.

Greezy Wheels was one of the higher-paid acts that year, but our set was mid-afternoon, the time of day when all smart Mexicans find shade and all dumb-ass hippies frolic in the sun. I was not among the latter group, despite my verifiable hippie credentials. It was all we could do to pull ourselves together and play a decent set amidst the swelter. We didn't see a lot of hope for an encore. There wasn't a lot of frolicking going on this day. In fact, most of the folks out there looked either dead or close to it. We never did get the body count.

When we looked to get our pay after the set, we were told we'd find Gino in his car—over "on that hill," a half-fucking-mile away. And he wasn't going to come to us. We had to walk to him. I was so hot by the time we got there, I was hallucinating that he was doing that old trick of pulling back a few feet, just as you reach for the door. I don't think he was—hard to tell—but I didn't put it past him. Either way, I was ready to strangle him when we sat down in the icy air-conditioned luxury car (so cold I could see my breath) and he half-sneered, as he handed us our money. A sneer? Really? A sneer? I really, really hate sneers. And I'm not even sure why he sneered. My guess is the dick tended to ooze out of him, and he couldn't really control it.

All in all, I forgive managers for being the way they are, although I still get queasy around parental units as managers (shudder). It's a tough gig that deals with mercurial personalities and impossible goals, and most artists are unmanageable anyway. When people assume I was Kinky Friedman's manager, I quickly correct them. I was his Executive Buttboy. Therefore, I could not be a dick.

Belushi was a Greezy Wheels fan

I know, hard to believe, but it's just another butt dial in a life filled with them. When I put the band on hiatus in 1978 and Mary and I vamoosed to NYC to work the Lone Star Cafe, I had little idea how big a change I had just made in my life. I was going from self-puffed rock-star snob to effete smart-ass club manager. I know that sounds like the same asshole, but it was a cataclysmic change for me. For one thing, I was to receive regular pay for being an asshole.

For another, I finally got a chance to reflect on the snob I'd left behind and enjoy the life that went on around me. I'd previously come to believe that life went on because of me, and not vice versa. I learned this from all the puffy snobs for whom I was now responsible on a nightly basis. And trust me, all of us who attain a level of stardom fall prey to puffery. Some more than others, but adulation is the prime source for puff.

I was a perfect manager for the times we were in, since I had had my little taste of rock stardom and I knew how to navigate egos. Whether it was fragile yet powerful egos

Life Is a Butt Dial

like Etta James or powerful yet paranoid egos like Yankees Manager Billy Martin (who, I swear, dusted off the chip on his shoulder every night on his way into the club), I never talked up or down to anyone, always straight at 'em, ego to ego. Yes, I admit it, I have a humongous ego. I will talk shit to anybody.

I knew when a star's request was reasonable or a possible felony. When a request bordered criminality, I alerted Mort, my direct boss, that "you don't want to know" what this hundred bucks is for, but "I'll handle it." Such was the case with our "big" Jay and the Americans show. I stress the word *big* because it wasn't really. Jay wanted it to be so, but he hadn't done a New York showcase in years, and it had been a long time since his hits. Unfortunately, he had quite a bit of puff still in him. Over-the-hill puff can be the most annoying of all.

Jay had received his full two days' pay as an advance, and when he only drew a couple hundred folks on his first night, he told Mort he wasn't coming in for the second night. Mort and his partner Bill went ballistic. If he didn't show, they were out plenty. His career may have been way past its prime, but his pay scale hadn't fallen as well. Naturally, I volunteered to go fetch him. Mary didn't call me Dudley Do-Right for nothing. I had a notion I could talk him into coming back. I also had a hundred bucks from Mort (*shhh!*), which I knew exactly how to use.

I happened to know Jay had a fondness for blow. So I got some.

Jay lived out in the deep wilderness of Brooklyn—I think it was Borough Park—in a row house with very little to distinguish it from any other house on the street, except that fucking Jay Black answered the door. He invited me into the kitchen to join him and several goombah-looking friends at the table, where we proceeded to march through the marching powder.

Meanwhile, his wife was having an I-shit-you-not Tupperware party in the front room. From the screams of laughter, it was hard to tell who had the best blow. I can't really remember how I convinced him to come back for the second show (I mostly let the blow do the talking), but he did. He made the gig. And I must say he killed it that night. Pretty sure he hit notes that only dogs could hear. Do-Right got his man—with a little help from the marching band.

John Belushi, at least in my experience, was the exact opposite of puffy. At night, he invariably shambled in a bit out of it, but always humble, sweet, and very much into the acts he came to see. Those acts were usually the older rhythm-and-blues greats that I had fat-armed Mort into adding into the Lone Star curriculum. John loved them all, and he always asked me quite shyly and politely if I would introduce him to the act of the evening, whether it be Johnny Shines or Big Joe Williams. Then he would fawn over his heroes like a schoolboy. Fawning beats puffing any day. He was adorable.

On one evening, Mort's booking assistant, Karen, jogged up to the second floor to tell me that Belushi was in the office we shared in the basement, and he needed something. When I got there, John was sprawled across Karen's chair in the center of the tiny office. He looked a little extra crispy, but he smiled and asked if I could float him enough for a hotel room; he'd lost his wallet. He said he needed four hundred bucks, which in those days probably also got him a good march, some Dom Perignon, and six or eight x-rateds in the room.

I took the money out of petty cash. I figured if Bill, the resident grinch, freaked, I'd cover it. And of course, Bill, the resident grinch, freaked the following morning. How the hell could I give "a fucked-up John Belushi our money"? Only Mort kept me from being fired on the spot. It did dawn on me briefly that John might forget—he was pretty wasted—and that I would have to cover what actually was a small fortune to Mary and me back then. But I had faith. And Belushi proved me right. That afternoon, John came in with his accountant and his agent, Mitch Glazer, walked straight over to me, and said, "I owe you money."

He did not look at all like the perpetually disheveled John I'd grown to know in the late-night hours. He was clean-shaved, nattily dressed in a full-length camel-hair coat and three-hundred-dollar touring cap, and all business. We crammed into my office, where the accountant whipped out four hundred-dollar bills, and we chatted about me almost being fired. Rather, John railed about it: He was truly pissed that Bill didn't trust him after "all he had done for the club." Which was an enormous amount. The Blues Brothers had had about eighty percent of their rehearsals at the club in the afternoons, and John had personally turned the SNL crew on to the joint. Once that crew knew about us, everybody knew. Everybody on the planet. Still, did I detect a trace of puff?

Whether I did or not, I didn't care two minutes later. His agent, Mitch Glazer, discovered that we had chatted over the phone several times about the Greezy Wheels. As he did, he exclaimed: "Hey John, you have Cleve's records. He's from Greezy Wheels."

And, for one endless-yet-too-soon-gone second, I was back to my old self-puffed rock-star-snobby me, an equal to the world's most famous Albanian American. John acknowledged that he did, indeed, have both of our London albums, and that he loved the band. My ego soared like a hawk.

He also said that from then on, if Bill gave me shit about anything, just let him know. I'm not sure what he could or would have done about anything, but I felt like I had a guardian angel. Belushi had my back, Jack.

I was nearly a Thirteenth Floor Elevator, believe it or not

Yeah, you can believe this one, even though I never even spoke to Roky or Tommy Hall about it. It was all Big Rikke's doing. Rikke had taken Roky under her wing in San Francisco, when Roky was at his most, shall we say, colorful. Pre-proper medications or long stays in the state's care, Roky was a free-bird whirlwind of nuts. He needed Rikke's wing, as much to ensure that he ate something everyday as to keep him from flying away with a band of pixies.

To that end, Rikke called me up in NYC and fairly demanded that my buddy Stephen and I come back to the left coast to join the Elevators. I had only departed the Haight a couple months prior, because someone had sold me a stolen airline ticket for fifty bucks (first class, no less), so I hadn't really reinvested in NYC. I was merely gallivanting, something many of us did in younger, freer days.

I immediately pigeonholed Stephen into it—he was a noted gallivanter as well. Stephen was already an accomplished bassist who'd had stints with Eric Andersen and a number of cool Village bands. I knew eight basic guitar chords and could play two sets of bongos simultaneously, but I had zero real rock skills at that time. Rikke knew I could organize the shit out of stuff, though, so maybe that was to be my gig: organize Roky. And, of course, Stephen and I were both tall and . . . cute.

As I reflect, it seems like we were back in the Haight within minutes of Rikke's call. It was a fast turnaround, but as we discovered, we needn't have hurried. Yes, Rikke was in command of the beloved flat at 408 Cole Street, and all was as normal as normal could be in the late Sixties, when there *was* no actual normal. But something was amiss. Roky. In the first couple weeks we were there, Roky was no more than a rumor or a scent in the wind, even though every Texan at Cole Street swore they saw him "just that morning," and he was "great."

I had earlier discovered a strange dynamic between Texans and New Yorkers when equal numbers of us shared the flat at 408. Both groups were used to big stuff. One giant state. One humongous city. Big stuff. But how we inhabited and perceived this largeness was quite different. We very often all ate dinner together sitting on the floor of one of the bedrooms, maybe five or six of each group. During a leisurely dinner, not one Texan would say a word. Not one New Yorker would shut up. It was a perfect communication system and why this New Yorker has been so comfy in Texas all these years.

It was also why I had to filter answers like "great" through several layers of what-the-fuck-does-that-mean before I had a clue where things stood. I found out where they stood when we next sat in our dinner semicircle and Roky surprised us by joining in. I realized it was the first time I had actually laid eyes on him. As the dinner was passed around, even the New Yorkers sat quiet. A plate of food sat before each of us, but nobody moved to eat it until Roky looked up from his plate, smiled perhaps the most angelic smile I shall ever see on any person, and smashed his lovely puss into his mashed potatoes. Before I could even get to what-the-fuck-does-that-mean, four Texans did exactly the same. We New Yorkers were stunned into silence, a five-hundred-year flood-plain type occurrence. Where things stood was *yikes*.

Um, okay then, band leader or mad cult messiah? We knew from cults, having discovered that the weird family that had occupied the flat at 407 Cole the summer before was the Manson bunch. We had seen into their world from our corner windows. Not pleasant. Off. Scary. Not shitting you.

This wasn't really a threatening gesture, though. What one does with one's mashed potatoes is a personal thing, and everyone had a good laugh about it. But it did dim the lights on my future as a bongo star. Not unpleasant. Not scary. Definitely off. Not shitting you.

The limited hope Rikke had had for discussing things with Tommy Hall had evaporated rather swiftly already. Tommy was loose even further afield than Roky, and whereas all Texans seemed to know where Roky was, the only thing being whispered about Tommy was that he had gone to the dark side—Scientology. Dark side, scientology: same thing. I never got to meet Tommy at all. Well, maybe I did, but I can't recall. He might have been standing next to his wife Clementine when I met her, but she was so glow-in-the-dark gorgeous it was hard to see anything else around her.

Stephen's and my hopes vaped totally on our next visit from Roky. About two weeks after the multiple potato face-plants, he burst up the stairs into the flat carrying a bottle of green dye, hollering that he was going to dye his hair green. He raced into the bathroom and locked himself in before Rikke or anyone could stop him. Pleas through the door to not dye anything rashly went unanswered, and for the next hour and a half, the sounds of water splashing, sloshing, and spilling into the apartment below filled the flat.

Finally, Roky emerged, unscathed, untouched by any trace of leprechaun anywhere. The bathroom, a different story. The entire room—everything—was green. Emerald City. By the time we surveyed the green-age, Roky was gone, along with any trace of the original Thirteenth Floor Elevators, or our chances to be a part of a resurrection. Fittingly, my career with the Elevators ended in the Green Room.

To this day, I am quite sure Roky had no idea what Rikke was up to. In fact, I'm pretty sure that he didn't know I was there, that I at one time aspired to play music with him, or that he helped point me toward Texas in the first place. When this never-was-a-gig fell through, Rikke had another brilliant never-to-be for me. I was going to fly to Texas on the gift ticket of a Texas pot dealer, start a band, and be her boyfriend. I was not apprised of that last item.

But that's another story. I can mention one thing: I was already pretty sure no electric jug players needed to apply for the gig. Never a fan.

Not every gig turns out as planned

There are many vagaries about the rock-and-roll lifestyle that change schedules, alter itineraries, and fuck with the fragile heads of every road manager who ever rode the bus. Forget knowing what's around the next corner. Sometimes you're struggling to *find* the next corner. Or you're looking for a chance to use the word *vagaries* just one more time in a sentence.

One of my most highly anticipated shows at the Lone Star Cafe was the coming of Larry Coryell. We were taking a chance on jazz at our little honky-tonk, and Larry was the first big name. Unfortunately, we had been closed down the night before for being over-crowded for a special weekend show with Johnny Winter. Our listed capacity was two hundred and twelve; there were nine hundred bodies in the room. We didn't see a problem with that.

The fire chief disagreed, demanding that we clear the house and shut our doors immediately. Teddy Slatus, Johnny's intrepid and often impossible manager (okay, he was an asshole), told them they could try to stop Johnny mid-set if they wanted, but he was not quite suicidal enough to do it himself. I also refused, pointing out that I was still a young man with so much to look forward to in life. Needless to say, the fire chief did not appreciate our zest for life. He had the place cleared within ten minutes of the end of the show and declared that we couldn't open our doors back up until the following Monday after a court appearance.

One of our owners, Bill Dick, who also had that Slatus kind of winning personality, decided we were going to open for Larry's show Sunday night, regardless. You know: Fuck them. Who do they think they are anyway? Which of course meant that it was possible I'd be hauled off to jail, because they knew who the fuck they were, and their badges fucking proved it. I actually didn't mind being the fall guy, since I was an ex-con and knew the ropes. I figured I'd just charge Bill double pay for every day behind bars.

They did not haul me off to double pay, but they did chase out what would have been a good crowd and close us back down less than fifteen minutes after opening, leaving just a few of our chosen friends—Larry, Joel Youngblood, and Doug Flynn of the New York Mets, two Playboy playmates, a bartender, Sweet Mary, myself and . . . Bo Diddley. Bo, who had just come in for a quick drink, also had a quick question: "Who the fuck is Larry Coryell?"

Larry knew who the fuck Bo was but apparently did not give a shit. His primary concern was the full bottle of Martell cognac sitting in front of him behind the bar. He started knocking back shots as soon as he knew the performance was canceled.

Bo, the baseball boys, and the babes all left after a couple rounds, leaving Mary, the bartender, and me in charge of Larry and the rapidly depleting bottle of Martell. Bo still hadn't figured out who Coryell was, but he totally didn't care. He was fucking Bo Diddley. He didn't have to know shit, and we loved him all the more for it.

Larry downed a few more shots, declaring after each, "One more round and I'm outta here."

A third of the way through the bottle, however, he suddenly declared he needed some blow to rev up for the road. We were pretty sure he wasn't going anywhere for a while—he could barely stand up by this point—but we did arrange for a gram to be dropped by the side door.

When I handed him the glassine, he dumped its entire contents on the bar. This would be the bar easily seen at any time through the front windows of the club. Fortunately, those contents didn't stay where they were long. With one fell snort, Larry vacuumed the bar clean, after which he stood straight up, completely erect . . . and keeled over backwards, landing flat on his back. Imagine, if you will, the remaining three of us staring down at him trying to decide if he was dead—and, if so, what we were going to do with the body. For a good two minutes, Larry looked as dead as any dead rock star we'd ever seen.

Finally, a gasp, snort, and dribble of snot proved that he was alive. Not cognizant, mind you, but alive. And definitely not going anywhere. Mary and I half-carried him upstairs to the dressing room and poured him onto the couch, that same couch that had seen so many nasty, disgusting things over its short life. I must say Larry looked quite beatific plotzed. Not nasty at all. Maybe a bit disgusting. You know, the snot bubble. Every hour or so for the next *eight* hours, Larry would sit up and holler, "Okay, point me to my car, and I'll be on my way."

After each declaration, we propped up the equally nasty and disgusting pillow and laid him back to rest. His snores echoed throughout the empty club.

Finally, at about six in the morning, we judged Larry fit enough to be let loose and handed him his keys. On his way out, he told us, "It's been real," before turning right, then left, then right again to go to his car.

And so ended our first big jazz show at the Lone Star.

Yeah, I was big in London—for about ten minutes

I had hooked Kinky up with the BBC to film a documentary about Texas roots music, and, lo, I became a star in the process. The piece took nearly two years to film, and it pretty much told the entire breathtaking Texas history of . . . accordions. I became a part of the actual filming when somebody delivered the "wrong Cadillac" to the shoot site, and Anthony Wall, the director/producer, decided, in a moment of indecipherable elliptical precision, that I was now needed in the scene. My theory is that they decided Kinky was too small for this Caddy and they needed my giant head to fill the screen. Whatever. I accepted my fate. This giant head has gotten me places.

The bits of film of us riding around Austin and bullshitting about various landmarks, people, and, of course, accordions became the shoelace for all the stories told throughout the program. So when they flew Kinky to London for its premiere on the telly, they flew me in too. They put us up at the super posh oh-my-god-do-people-really-live-like-this Langham Hotel, wherein interviews commenced immediately. Kinky was his normal surly self, and the London press loved it. Kinky's surliness, my giant head—we both know how to get by in life.

Unbeknownst to me, the folks at the Beeb had decided to invite a second cousin of mine to tea with me. My cousin could have been a second or a hundredth cousin, for all I knew (how would I know who was fucking whom back then?), but he happened to be the quite powerful leader of the Labor Party at the time, Roy Hattersley. A formal invite was sent from the high mucky at BBC to high mucky Roy, but when a secretary turned down the request, instead of Roy, himself, all hell broke loose in the media. Apparently mucky-mucks are supposed to speak for themselves. Or the Brit media will speak to everybody.

Nearly every daily paper carried a condemnation of Roy for having so rudely snubbed his "bastard American cousin," making me the top item of the day. Which only deepened the Kinkster's surliness. He absolutely hated that I was getting more press than he that morning. His mood carried into the afternoon, when I had scheduled a lunch with a top editor at Faber & Faber Publishing. Kinky didn't yet have a book deal for the UK, and they were ready to offer. We met the very aristocratic and charming editor at a private writers and publishers club, a staid, quiet, trés exclusive joint, and almost immediately the mood thickened. When I used a "royal we" to answer a question about the then-current state of Kinky's publishing in the U.S., Big Dick exploded.

I'd probably have diffused things had I not been introduced to the horrors of cilantro only moments before. I had never tasted it, I hated tasting it, and I never wanted to taste it again, and I know I am exactly like fifty percent of the population when I say this. Kinky's explosion came as I was desperately trying to rake the nasty out of my mouth, à la Tom Hanks in "Big." I became furious, cilantro furious. I ended up spitting it out at Kinky, as we both jumped out of our chairs and our escalating argument rose to near screams. It was brutal, one of the worst fights Kinky and I ever had, but ya never know how people are going to view these kinds of things. Nobody in the room even acknowledged our presence. Evidently, writers and publishers did this shit all the time. The editor made the deal offer on the spot. Guess she liked it rough.

And Kinky's surliness finally subsided the next afternoon, when Townes Van Zandt and Guy Clark walked in on a record-store appearance midtown. London was suddenly thick with Texas. As it was already evening, we all decided to take Texas to the nearest Irish bar, The Mean Fiddler, where we commandeered the booth next to the stage and started swapping tales. The Fiddler was known for being a tough Irish bar, probably the toughest bar in London. We wanted to see if it was Texas tough. The cute little acoustic trio chirping on stage pretty much vanquished that thought.

Townes had taken antabuse, which made him so intense he was leaving finger marks in the wooden tabletops, and all of us were talking at max volume. In my experience, Guy's speaking voice always stood out. He just had a bigger barrel of a chest than most. It wasn't that he was so loud; he was just . . . imperial. Townes's volume soared when he and I started reminiscing about one of his great loves in life, the late Linda Miller. At the same time, Kinky and Guy were arguing over something about which neither Townes nor I cared. Four guys hollering at the same time—not the rhythm section that trio had envisioned for later touring.

And the thing about Americans yelling at each other is that we never fucking quit. Texans are decidedly American on this account. The caterwaul continued unabated until the bartender, who actually did look like he could kick all four of our skinny asses, eighty-sixed us. We were firmly and swiftly hustled out the door, kicked out of the toughest bar in London. Yes, a major coup. Kinky and I chuckled over this the entire cab ride back to Hotel de Luxe. I had learned an important lesson here. The Irish don't put up with Texas shit. I like that.

Kinky's set at a top London club the next night, his only live performance of the week, was a total sellout. Everyone sang along with their favorite tunes, and we had a nice sit down with Van Morrison backstage. On the following night, Saturday, "A Texas Saturday Night" ran for four-and-a-half hours on the BBC, with two intermissions. We watched it at Anthony Wall's house after bangers and brew in his backyard. Bangers are like taste-free Polish sausage, but the brew makes you not care. Kinky had a lovely time watching and talking about himself for four-and-a-half hours, which he will readily admit is a passion.

It was a great documentary, a ninety-minute version of which aired later on PBS (none of my scenes were cut, which extended my ten minutes of fame to twelve minutes of fame). At that time, it was the fifth-most-watched documentary in BBC history. Kinky maintains that we should view this with some skepticism, averring that the fourth-most-watched documentary in BBC history was "Butterflies of Uganda." Fuck it—I got my twelve minutes.

The Lone Star Cafe was the shit

Of course, I speak of the one in New York City, not the small chain of Texas restaurants that were decidedly not the shit. For a good while in the Seventies and Eighties, it was the center of Texas culture in New York, if such a thing actually existed. Culture, it was. Texas, I'm not so sure.

Texas ex-pats in New York and even ones just visiting were even more annoying than Texans in Texas (and we all know how annoying our fellow Texans can be). Most felt the Lone Star owed them a fealty, as they were the "real" representatives of the great state, and we were just . . . not. So, when they bellowed their way into the club demanding special treatment, we treated them with an extra touch of douche bag. You know, to make them feel more at home.

We did become an official embassy of the state while I was there, and we did bring in an amazing assortment of Texas acts, but there was a whole lot of not-Texas going on there too. One of my favorite not-Texas things was Robert Gordon. Not that Robert is a thing, but he had this . . . thing. It was rockabilly to the max, but it was also something beyond. He could easily have headlined a bar in Star Wars, his stuff was so of the moment.

At the Lone Star, he never had anyone but the best players, notably Chris Spedding and Danny Gatton in succession on guitar (and on at least one occasion, both at the same time). Every show was fucking hair-raising. And I so envied his hair. Never has there been a more perfect pompadour.

I always arranged my schedule to be there for Robert's shows, despite the fact he drove me nuts every time he brought in his stadium-sized I-gotta-fucking-have monitors. For our postage-stamp-size stage. We had a Lone Star Cafe reunion a couple years ago, and I managed to cajole Robert into playing it. His last comment, before we rung off with a deal: "Monitors, man. Monitors." We gave him monitors. He killed it.

That people who came to the Lone Star were actually getting a hybrid New York/Texas experience—and not an unadulterated cowboys, tumbleweeds, and John Wesley Harding experience—never really mattered. They came anyway. Magical things happened there. Sometimes the people themselves provided the magic.

One afternoon we got a call from the Secret Service letting us know the king was coming. Naturally we inquired, "Which king?"

We were not aware the king of Spain was in town, but we jumped to attention when they informed us they were sending a team of agents over to check us out the following day.

I believe my first duty was to make sure nobody was carrying any drugs, guns, or pornography. I confiscated the former and the latter. None of us had a gun. We were smart enough to know we'd probably use it on a Texan someday.

The agents did scope out the club very thoroughly, and on the following night we prepped our premier table at the center of the balcony overlooking the stage for King Juan Carlos and Queen Sophia. The tables on either side were to be kept empty, and the guys who actually had the guns would discreetly surround him from behind.

At exactly the appointed time, a limo pulled up to the revolving door and a truly elegant couple stepped out to be escorted directly to the table by our uber-efficient staff. We sat them with great pomp and circumstance. They were charming, beautifully dressed, handsome to the toes. They were not the king and queen. Uber-staff had just seated our general manager's dentist and his wife at the king's table.

And just in time, the real king and queen arrived thirty seconds later. The Secret Service guys were about to go ballistic—I'm pretty sure one of them may have even reached for his piece as they tried to yank the dentist and wife out of their chairs—but Juan Carlos was a pretty smooth guy for a king, and he invited the dentist to join them at the table.

The next day, the incident hit Page Six in the *New York Post*, the ultimate NYC gossip page. It reported that the king, queen, and their "very good friends," the dentist and his wife, were seen out and about the night before. I'm betting the king got a free cleaning out of it.

The Doors: Rock-and-Roll Hall of Fame or dumpster fire?

A Facebook friend has recently asked in a post if the Doors were not, in fact, the worst band of all time. A good many folks have said yes, they were, which kinda surprised me. I was much more in the corner of those who responded by saying Rush was history's true dumpster fire, but I do have to say the Doors were both of the above—legit hall-of-famers and godawful. It just depends on which end of their career you got to see. I witnessed both ends. I am torn.

I first saw (and met) Morrison and the Doors at a tiny little joint called Ondine that sat under the Manhattan side of the 59th Street Bridge in NYC. It was just after the release of their first record, and I only knew about them because I worked in accounting at their publishing company. Yeah, go figure: me, accounting.

Their album had come to us before its release, and I had the chance to take it into the listening booth. These guys were a lot darker than the shit coming out of the Bay Area, but there was something pleasantly sinister about them. Pleasantly sinister was a good thing. It somehow prepared us for the truly sinister shit going on at the time. You know, 'Nam, Nixon, dark matter—the real sinister.

When I discovered the Ondine gig only weeks later, I hit the joint in my left-coast best: my fringe jacket, fringe boots, and a studied insouciance. I was one of maybe ten folks there, and all ten of us were fully blown up. The band was nails, the stage rocked with feral energy, and Morrison was as beautiful and magnetic as any human I had ever seen. Maybe even as beautiful as Hendrix. Mr. Too Cool for School would have left about halfway through the set, but I was riveted, before I bolted. I had never seen anything like it. Where was the fucking bass player? I stayed. And I told Morrison that he'd changed my life, that I was going to the Haight the following week. That was only half true: I was going to the coast, but I wanted him to know how much I dug their stuff. And that I was not at all insouciant.

I didn't run into Morrison until a couple years later, when I was hanging out in LA with Eric Andersen and his band, which included my pals Stephen and Andy. Warner Brothers had put Eric and band up in a mansion on the hill while they recorded Eric's "Avalanche" album. I had declared myself road manager and moved into a vacant granny suite in the basement.

On one afternoon with no sessions planned, a game of water tag commenced in the oh-yeah-this-is-Hollywood pool. Morrison, who was visiting Eric (Eric knew fucking everybody, still does), joined the game, which flowed along as a water-tag game might—until Jim got tagged. When he did, the action stopped. Completely. Jim had to decide whom he should tag. Evidently, decisions like this were a problem. As, apparently, was leaving the stage.

He mounted the diving board and strutted imperiously back and forth, doing a kind of LA meets Mick Jagger chicken prance. By the time he chose his victim—who else but the most beautiful woman there, Eric's wife, (the late) Debbie Green—the game was pretty much over.

After we all got dressed, we hung out in the living room until Morrison passed out drunk sitting up on the couch. We spent about twenty minutes touching his snakeskin pants and wondering if we should wake him, before bugging out for some burgers down on Sunset. He was gone when we got back.

And his shows were gone by that time as well. There was only an actor playing the role of Jim Morrison anymore. The band had limited energy by itself. They needed Jim to be real, and he'd lost touch with real. At the last show I caught, at the Santa Clara Pops Festival, people laughed when he fell oh so dramatically to the stage floor. He had become bloated, jaded, the worst of LA—and unacceptable. He was a caricature of what he had been. A caricature could not carry the Doors.

I prefer to remember the band I saw at Ondine, the one that was cooler than my fringe jacket. But I did learn one thing from my brushes with the Doors: I was not going to make a very good road manager.

I see dead people

Okay, not like Haley Joel What's-His-Name. I cannot see the victim of your soon-to-be axe murderer standing next to you, nor is your dead father confessing anything sordid to me. However, I do see folks I knew. I see them in my thoughts and dreams, and, yes, they do speak to me.

For the last two weeks the two loudest voices have been those of Johnny Paycheck and Joseph Heller. If there was ever a more disparate pair, I am unaware (yes, I also dream in rhyme). Johnny was possibly the most tornadic personality I ever met, with the exception of maybe Jaco Pastorius. Both inhaled enormous amounts of marching powder, but Jaco hasn't visited in a while, so more on him later—when he checks in.

Johnny is still apologizing to me for the last crazy thing he pulled on me one night at the Lone Star Cafe. He called in from the road somewhere, said he was passing through NYC, and asked if I would mind if Sandy Alexander dropped off an ounce of blow with me that he could pick up the next day. And oh, by the way, he'd already told Sandy to do it.

Sandy, though a reasonable sort, was also the president of the New York chapter of the Hells Angels and could be scary as shit when scary as shit was called for. Within an hour of the call, Sandy stopped by with the goodies. Neither he nor I was totally pleased with the process, so when he departed, I only took the smallest taste of the goods—quality assurance, of course. And then Paycheck never showed up. He didn't call either.

Sandy was not pleased. I could hear scary as shit in his voice on the phone, but I had to return the baggy. An ounce of blow was beyond both my means and my desires (probably why I still sit here). However, I was so paranoid of having tasted the product—that the loss would be noticed—I bought a full gram of it from another friend to replace it, maybe fifteen times the amount I had tasted. Sandy was still not pleased to have to fetch it back, but at least we didn't visit Scary-as-Shitville.

Joe Heller couldn't have presented a more opposite demeanor and view of life than Johnny's. Maybe it was just the fact Joe was lying in bed for the first few conversations we had on the phone—we got to know each other while he was recovering from Guillain-Barre syndrome—that our chats were so contemplative, so charmingly genteel.

I know his daughter has issues with this view of her dad—there were big problems there—but that's the Joe I knew until the end. He actually credited me with saving his life through those phone calls, though I think more credit is due to his nurse, Valerie, whom he later married.

Kinky and I last saw Joe and Valerie at their place out at the ass end of Long Island, where he lived the life of a beloved baird among the rich and obnoxious. No doubt, he was an upgrade for Amagansett. Unlike Johnny, who visits whenever he feels like it, I nearly always ask Joe to drop by, always hoping there is a nugget of wisdom or advice I had forgotten of which he can remind me. I know my shock of white hair gives me a kind of Heller-esque image, but I can only dream of ever writing anything as good as his best. C'mon, Joe, give me a clue.

My Vietnam

When I was drafted in 1966, I knew that since I had no discernible skills coming out of high school other than dribbling a basketball and forging my mother's signature, I'd be sent straight to the front if I passed the physical.

Luckily, I did not. Okay, luck had little to do with it. For that first call-up, I stayed up on speed for four days without bathing or changing my clothes. My undies were a delight by day four. When they took my blood and told me to hold a cotton over the puncture, I did not, and I bled all over my filthy white shirt. This got me a fast-forward to the shrink.

As I sat at his desk trying to answer questions I could barely hear through the whine of the amphetamine haze, I let my eyes run amok. I had an astigmatism and had discovered I could make them wiggle noticeably, not unlike disturbed jello. Pretty sure the eyes did it: He sent me home, said they'd give me a holler the next year. I was the only one of about four hundred guys who got the free pass home that morning.

I got my second call-up one year later in Oakland. This

time, there were more guys waiting to see the shrink than those already being fitted for their combat boots. Yikes. And I had only stayed up one night. Worse, some of the other guys had far more sophisticated presentations of their unfitness.

One guy was doing handstands in the middle of the room; another was inviting all of us to join him and hit up speed in the bathroom. I'm thinking the former may have taken up the latter's offer. However, both were sent back to the induction line, where a Marine welcomed them to "the shit."

I was sure my feeble little wiggly eyes act was doomed, but the shrink must have found me more believable a nut job than the two preceding nut jobs, and he cut me loose again ("see you next year, soldier").

Not believing my dumb luck, I decided to split for Texas immediately and go to work in a field for which I felt I was by then fully qualified: smuggling pot. I figured flying shit over America to be a much more productive career than being in the shit for America.

And it almost worked. I was busted on my third trip from Texas to New York. I say "almost" because I was then no longer eligible to be sent into the shit. That I served eleven months of a seven-year stretch in Huntsville is of little significance. Given the choice of burning some shit or burning up in the shit, always go with burning some shit.

Harry Dean

HD never acted like a star, as far as I know. He just liked to attach himself to the moment, whatever that moment might be. You didn't have to be a fellow star to be that moment, which is how I know this. I met him when I toured Australia with Kinky Friedman and former *Daily News* columnist Mike McGovern.

HD was huge down under and was touring there with, among others, Billy Swan and James Intveld in his band. Harry Dean fancied himself a country singer, and he wasn't half-bad. He was about half-good. A lot of Kinky's and HD's shows were double-bills, so we were often all at the same hotel.

McGovern had come up with some Aussie pot that was so good that we had a single ounce of it flown in to Sydney from Perth, three thousand fucking miles away. Harry loved pot, and we loved getting him as high as we could with that pot. He attached himself to whoever rolled the joints—usually me.

On at least three of these occasions, the rest of us went

out for coffee or food, each time leaving Harry Dean outside whichever room we'd all been in. I guess once stoned, he became the moment. So he meandered off, each time staying away at least an hour.

On every occasion, when we returned, we'd find Harry Dean wandering aimlessly around the atria or outside the rooms. Lost. He couldn't find or remember his room number. We had a routine by the third time this happened: I asked him for his key, noted the room number on that key, and led him to it.

A couple years later, Kinky and I were at the Cinegrill in the Roosevelt Hotel in LA, where Kinky was doing two nights of shows (legendary ones, I might add).

At one point, I leaned over to whisper to Kinky that I was going upstairs to burn one between shows and headed across the lobby to the elevators. As I stepped into the already-open doors, I felt a ghostly presence slip in behind me: Harry Dean. Don't know how (or if) he heard my whisper—didn't even know he was there that night—but he smiled and asked, "Going my way?"

So we burned through a fatty, chatted a bit up in my room. When we left, I turned toward the elevator and he turned the other way, saying he had to do something. I told him I'd see him downstairs, he said he'd be down in a minute. Didn't see him for another two years. Harry Dean was always the moment.

Yes, backstage is better

Okay, maybe not to everyone's tastes. If you're coming for laser lights, exploding monitors, pomp and circum-fucking-stance, you may disagree, but take my word for it: Backstage is a special place. It's the DMZ between reality and surreality.

Folks enter from the outer world as normal slugs carrying guitars, drumsticks, and whatnot and transform into superstars as they prance to center stage. I know this because I once pranced. In between the slug walk and the prance is a rarefied universe that offers moments to a select few witnesses. The moments are almost never recorded, but they are historical to the extreme.

To whit: Kinky Friedman and Abbie Hoffman in the Lone Star Cafe dressing room demanding that I listen to them both tell me the same joke at the same time and tell them who sold it better. They both sucked, which was weird, as Kinky has great delivery and Abbie could easily have done stand-up. I guess jokes should always just be listened to in mono. Stereo fucks with the beat.

There are levels of insanity in backstages. I fully believe that all performers, especially the great ones, suffer from one form of insanity or other. It comes with the territory—especially the backstage territory.

On one extreme, I present the Scruggs Family Band. On the night they played the Lone Star in my charge, a young fiddler named Jana Jae was opening their show. Jana put on a pretty good show, so when she pleaded with me to ask the Scruggs if she could sit in with them, I agreed. I wouldn't have normally, but I have learned from a long and lovely marriage to one that helping women fiddlers is good juju.

I took her up to their dressing room and ducked my head in respectfully—to the quietest, most somber backstage I'd ever seen. The Scruggs were seated in a semicircle, hands folded in their laps, in complete silence. No one spoke to me. No one even looked at me.

I paused to assess whether or not the entire family had had a stroke before asking weakly if they'd mind having Jana sit in for a tune or two. One head turned to me—Earl's—and said, "We don't do no set-ins."

Period. Not another word came forth. Jana, of course, was crushed. She was standing right next to me. I was more confused than anything else. Was the rest of the family still stroked out?

Robin Williams, who popped in regularly to see Kinky, was just a tad more kinetic than the Scruggs. One of his more infamous Lone Star cameos put him on stage with Don Imus for a furiously hilarious ten minutes of dueling reverends, but my first direct experience with him involved blow and mathematics, not to mention electricity.

He always bounced in wearing his trademark suspenders/pseudo-mime outfit, and on this occasion, Billy the bartender brought him downstairs to my office and asked if he could turn Robin on to a blast in the privacy of my lair. I of course allowed that he could, as long as I got a taste.

Billy agreed and laid out three lines on my desk. Big lines. Very good shit. Robin sat down, proceeded to do two of them, and immediately apologized with, "Whoops, I guess I miscounted."

He then gazelled up the steps to the main floor, jumped on stage, and spit-fired the most hysterical (if not, indeed, historical) fifteen minutes of insanity never recorded for posterity. Easily a thousand volts. Mega wattage. I'm pretty sure about half the audience laughed themselves into real strokes. I now knew where Mork got his rocket fuel.

If you're going to get popped, choose your companions well

If you are with one of your pals when the flashlight hits your face and the badge blinds you, you may not fare so well. You will soon be sharing handcuffs instead of tokes in the back seat of a Crown Victoria. If you are with, say, the pope smoking a fatty, your chances of sailing a charge are considerably better. It's always good to be with a pope at your popping. I know this because I have been at some poppings that actually turned out okay.

My first experience with getting away with one occurred at a long-defunct NYC club called Cheetah. And well it should be defunct: It was the first disco in New York, and as my friends all know, I consider a disco to be the first floor down on the elevator to Hell. No greater evil has ever been devised for a serious touring musician . . . except maybe a Grateful Dead cover band, which actually could be two levels down.

I was at this bungalow-on-the-Styx because Wilson

Picket was there, and I was there to meet him. He was supposed to do a lip-synch set for the glassy-eyed throng witlessly cavorting through the strobe lights. I was there on a mission, a mission very much like my every mission. Right—it was a cannabis rescue operation, only this time I was not the victim of sobriety. Wilson was. He couldn't fucking believe he had to perform for this decidedly un-captivated audience. I found him fuming about his agent backstage.

I leaped into action. The signs of fuckingagentosis were clear, even in the dark. Wilson needed to be toxed, and I had the toxing device, a well-crafted doob. I lit it up as I walked up, and handed it to Wilson. No more than three jolts in, the flashlight appeared, followed by a uniformed beat cop. The light caught me mid-toke. Years later, whenever a follow spot hit me on stage, I would have the same instant of terror I felt that night. That moment when you say to yourself, "Jesus, I really have to pee," then realize you just did.

There was no doubt this guy was going to bust us. Off-duty (which he was) or not, a good bust was a good bust. Beat cops don't get a lot of those. But when he realized I was standing with Wilson "Get-the-Fuck-Outa-Here" Pickett, he dead-stopped and said: "Oh, Mr. Pickett. I didn't see you there. Please excuse me."

And he left. OMG, we weren't gonna get popped. Wilson smiled that all-tooth smile of his, took the roach from me, and re-lit it. We finished the joint. Neither one of us said another word until he headed out to the stage. I didn't stay for the show. I needed a change of underwear.

Getting busted by Bill Graham was even scarier than a real bust. Not that he was a bad guy or didn't support our countercultural ideas. He was really a fairly congenial sort, but one thing he demanded was that we didn't smoke dope or do other drugs at the Fillmore East. We obeyed Bill's rules. We knew that if he caught you smoking something other than a Lucky Strike, he might literally drag you out to the street by the hair and kick you in the ass before he fired you. We'd seen him chase customers out all the way from the stage to the front door swinging a mic stand, over minor disagreements. Bill pretty much always scared the shit out of us by simply being Bill. Ah yes, angels we were—when Bill was in town. When he wasn't? Not so much.

We were all hippies in one way or another, and a ticket to the counterculture required frequent, shall we say, *grokking*. The best groks occurred around the best drugs. And the Fillmore staff always had access to the best drugs. Of course, we were required once again by countercultural rules of etiquette to both share our shit and thumb our nose at the Establishment. When Bill was in town, he was our beloved boss. When he was out of town, he was the Establishment. So we often shared our shit on premises. It's all about the grok, y'all. And, you know, fuck the Establishment.

After long negotiations and much Deadhead angst, Bill finally brought the Grateful Dead to the Fillmore for a four-day run. It was a big fucking deal. He paid them enough that they bought new cars for every single member of their family, like about twenty-five folks at the time. I did love that about the Dead. They were a fantastic example of what options are open to people who very seriously want to counter the inherited culture. I had lived near them in the Haight, had been to several shows in the Bay Area (mostly free stuff), and had grokked with a couple of them backstage. Did I like their music? Not so much.

On the first day of the four-day run, I went on stage to say hello to some of the guys as they set up for sound check. As I passed Jerry Garcia, he handed me a joint—now see *that's* what I liked about them. Once again following the hard-and-fast Rule of Hippie, I stopped to help him finish it. It didn't matter that Bill was in town: The hard-fast is such that when a Grateful Dead hands you a joint, you grok it down to the roach. This time we were about done with it before Bill pulled up behind Jerry. The haze was hanging blue in the air over me, the about-to-be-dragged-out-by-the-hair jobless hippie.

Once again, the shining star that was my joint mate saved me. The Dead could do that. They trumped all rules. They owned the subculture, the one upon which Bill Graham so heavily relied at the Fillmore. For that one brief moment in time, I also owned it. Jerry and me, brothers of the bush and more powerful than Bill's terrifying bushy eyebrows. I bolted as soon as Bill's attention shifted to the monitor mix. I did catch the show, but passed on the remainder of the week. There wasn't enough room at the front of the stage for the customary topless acid dancers that accompanied so many of the San Francisco shows. Without the topless acid dancers . . . not so much.

It isn't writ in stone that your ganja companions must be stars to avoid shit. Sometimes it's another kind of influence that diffuses a situation. Once the Greezy Wheels began touring out of state, one of our favorite stops was Oxford, Mississippi. Not because the statue in the town square of a Confederate soldier is called the "Trophy for Second Place," but because, for decades, Oxford has been the home of the official U.S. government pot farm, housed at the Ole Miss campus. Take away the statue, the frat rats, and several hundred years of history, and this could be my favorite city in the whole world.

Lo and behold, high-grade pot was readily available throughout the town, and on our first visit, nearly half of Oxford showed up to our gig. The owner of the club, whose name and name of the club I cannot remember, introduced us in particular to one guy said to have the best pot in the state. On our first break we invited him onto the tour bus, our trusty 1949 Flxible Flyer, which Tracy had had to park facing the wrong way on the street outside the club. We proceeded to grok the shit out of our new friend's shit, until the smoke was billowing out of the half-opened windows.

Apparently the Fates were also high on whatever Panama Red hybrid we were smoking. A bubble top appeared in front of us, lights flashing. We all freaked in unison and started squirting ozium all over the place. To no avail. The billowing continued. The smoke was pea-soup thick. The cop exited his car and approached our door. The owner of the weed jumped up and hollered: "Not to worry, y'all. I've got this."

He met the trooper at the door, at which time we heard the cop say, "Oh . . . It's you, Mr. Mayor. My mistake."

So here's my advice: If you're looking for a great buzz in Oxford, try the city council first.

Yes, it's true: I have been in more than one band

Though I have spent two-thirds of my life known as founder and leader of Greezy Wheels, I have whored around a little in the music world. Not that the whoring made me any money. The world of the musician whore is, for the most part, not one of riches and glory. Some whores do make it big, most do not, but if we are true to our pimp—the music itself—we can justify all the blow jobs we gave out trying to make it. It's always about that funky music . . . white boy.

The first band I ever became a part of was (almost) formed at the Fillmore East. It coalesced around a twelve-year-old kid named Sean. Usually, the only things that coalesce around twelve-year-olds are pimples, but this kid was different. He could play the guitar. He was, in fact, a phenom, so good that he was once invited to join Jeff Beck on stage, where he killed it with a note-for-note version of "Jeff's Boogie." The kid was a fucking tape recorder. I got the impression Jeff was not thrilled with having played with a tape recorder.

Anyway, we teamed up with a kid not much older than Sean named Lotus and declared ourselves a band. I believe we had all of two rehearsals on the Fillmore mezzanine before Sean asked me to come uptown with him and meet "his manager," a guy named Steve Paul. Steve Paul had found fame with his club, Steve Paul's Scene, which was quite the scene for maybe two years. Jam sessions were the evening menu, and everyone who was anyone sat in on that stage at some point. Stephen even got to sit in with Hendrix one night. What I got was the pleasure of meeting Steve Paul, who, as I would soon learn, was all about . . . Steve Paul.

For that brief moment in time, Steve Paul was also Johnny Winter's manager, so I was cautioned by Sean to pay attention and be respectful. Right. Like I was going to let a twelve-year-old kid tell me what to do.

I was street hip, well prepared for just about anything, even at that young age. Yeah, ready for anything. Anything except a guy with an attitude wearing a kimono. I did not dare or care to discover if he had anything on underneath it. I suppose, if he had been hunky, I might have ventured a peek. You know, to gauge shit.

Steve Paul was anything but hunky. To be kind, call him chunky, but you don't get the full picture until you include greasy (as in hair) and sweaty (as in everything else). His 'tude was a cross between Julius fucking Caesar and Pope Pius XII. You know, imperious rex, holier than thou, with a whole lot of fuck-you-I'm-rich. I have no idea how he convinced Johnny he should be his manager. Johnny was blind. Maybe he didn't notice the kimono.

Steve's sitting area was arranged so he sat a full head taller than anyone else. He virtually commanded you to look up at him at all times. I was having a hard time with this. I was pretty sure I was starting to turn to stone. Something evil here lurked. It predated Jabba the Hut, but it had to have been of the same bloodline.

He was offering us the world too. The plan was to let us live on a ranch he and Johnny had rented in Upstate New York and rehearse the band into shape. He would feed us, keep us in pot, and we were pretty sure there would be groupies. Unfortunately, all of the above was not enough to convince me this would work. Steve Paul was that weird. His offerings of rock fantasies terrified me. I cannot fully describe why, except, to this day, kimonos give me nightmares.

I begged out of the band on the way to the subway that night, wished Sean the best, and never looked back.

Though there are a couple other non-Greezy bands that I have graced with my presence, beyond a doubt the one that most shaped my current self was the Walls Unit Rodeo Band, my prison band. You know, one of those bands in which members all wear the same suits, except they're all striped. I actually didn't mind. The stripes added a good twenty pounds to my still-model-slender frame. One does not covet a model-slender frame in the slam, unless one covets a boyfriend.

Every weekend in October in Huntsville, Texas, the convicts would participate in a full-on rodeo in an arena right outside the prison walls. This meant you could opt to be trampled by a pissed-off ball-cinched bull as you tried to grab a prize tied to the bull's horns. I cannot tell you how much fun it was to *not* participate in this. Or you could volunteer to ride one of those suckers, which also meant you were going to be trampled by a pissed-off ball-cinched bull. Even more fun to avoid.

Luckily, I did not have to contemplate such doings. I was named to the Walls Unit band, the best band in the entire prison system. It turns out the wardens had a competition each year to field the best band for the rodeo, and ours managed to pry an amazing guitarist out of another unit, right under the nose of his rival. This guy had the Chet Atkins thing tight, and he could sing. His version of "Silver Wings" still pops into my inner jukebox every now and then. He was about to parole out on a dime for kiting checks, but the warden was already plotting to keep him in the full ten years. This fuck wanted to have the best band every year. Contemplate that.

Our rhythm section was a canvass of jailhouse tats and greased ducktails. Both the bassist and drummer were doing life for murder. Oddly, despite looking like street-corner thugs, they were not the scariest-looking guys in the band. The guitarist earned that award. He was pleasant, soft-spoken, and had an endearing smile. Serial killer all the way.

Each Saturday and Sunday in October, we striped up (we normally wore all white inside), picked up our instruments in the library, and headed out the front door. The stage was already set, by whom I had no clue, right next to it, and we kicked off the day with about a half-hour of song, no dance. Gee, fun. "Also, do not look suggestively at anyone, do not move suggestively in any way, and do not talk to anybody." How the fuck was I going to communicate with my adoring fans? My voice may be adequate, but it's these beady hazel eyes that make it all happen.

We were then marched around to the rodeo arena and forced to slog through the muck to a stage on a flatbed truck at its center. The guard who'd marched us in plugged us into something and told us to face forward. I chuckled under my breath. The bull was the roadie. Perfect. I toyed with sending him for fresh towels until the rodeo announcer barked: "And that was Johnny Bailey on Nightmare, ladies and gents. Too bad Johnny got bucked, but don't worry, y'all. Johnny's got twenty-five more years to work on it." Yeah, a real comedian.

I decided to ask for the towels. Fuck it. A week in the shitter would have been worth it. But when I turned to cause some shit, the stage moved. Rather, it rotated left, and the guard told us to start playing. The guitarist, who had seen me fuming, launched into "Stagger Lee," one of my big numbers, usually reserved for the end of the set. The show went on, I let the roadie off the hook, and we did a herky-jerky three-sixty another four times before our set ended. I thanked my guitar slinger. He had taught me a valuable lesson: Don't fuck with your roadie. He controls the ground switch.

I did join one other group while in the slam, the men's choir (you were expecting co-ed?). This is because the very first thing a drive-up acquires is religion. Okay, it's the second thing. The first is his story about how he is innocent, in fact had been railroaded, and is appealing his case to the highest level. Not a single person in the joint is guilty. That "highest level" would have been another convict, a guy named Danny, the unit writ writer and jailhouse lawyer.

Danny, a lifer, was so prolific in rep-ing other cons' cases from inside that the warden didn't dare deny him an office—which was, as it happened, in the basement of the church. So, in order, the newbie acquires a new lawyer and then heart-felt-God-fearin' religion. He goes to church for both. And if you believe that shit about heart-felt, I do have a bridge or two in my portfolio I'm looking to divest.

The Night Owl Cafe was home to an amazing group of musicians, from Fred Neil to the Lovin' Spoonful to Sopwith Camel to James Taylor. Getting to be there was a great start to a life of musical depravity and manic depression. I have not regretted one second of that life. The awning in the background on the other side of the street would later become the Blue Note. The epicenter of hip has always been this very corner.

This is the Fugitives, the first band that allowed me to haunt them at the Night Owl and other places. To the left are the Charmatz brothers, Evan and Ray, who later became the Chandler brothers. Center right, we have Tom 'Tommy Joe' Johanson, the lead guitarist. On the right is Phil Feliciotto, who changed his name to Cody and wrote a bunch of hits with Neil Sedaka (thanks for the photo, Phil). This photo, unlike many of their publicity shots, shows how cute they were. The bevy of seventeen-year-old girls who haunted them readily agreed. Ray briefly dated Shelley Plimpton, who later starred in the original production of *Hair* and spawned Martha Plimpton.

Ah yes: the One Knite, site of my first gig other than at a tempura restaurant. A sleazier, yet homier joint you will never find anywhere. Tastefully decorated with everything from garbage cans to car parts hanging from the ceiling, painted throughout with my fave spring color—flat black—it spawned a whole bunch of us. In the center is Roger 'One Knite' Collins, the face of the darkness within. Would you buy a beer from this man? Fuck yeah. The bottom left photo tells it like it was virtually any night of the week. The bottom right photo, taken outside the club, is of the legendary Angela Strehli on the left and Emma Little (who still owns the hearts of half the men in Austin) on the right—and features my first co-headliner, Jimmie Vaughan, then fronting the band Storm. Okay, co-headliner might be a little strong . . .

Photo by Sammy Mack Royal

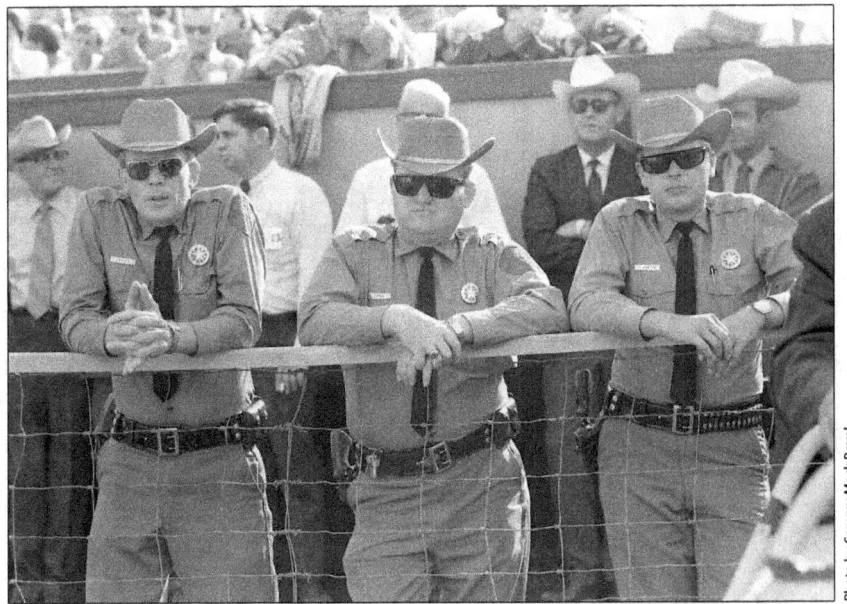

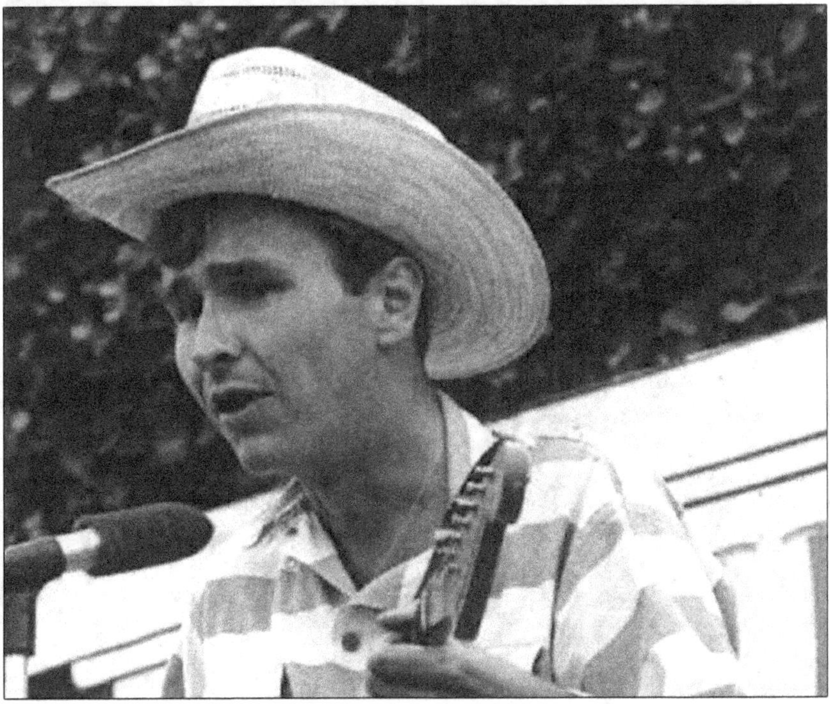

Huntsville Prison Rodeo, 1973—my turn to star. Oh, yay. Here I am singing my big number, 'Stagger Lee,' for our opening set outside the front door of the Walls Unit. The top photo is of my prison posse. Pretty sure the one in the center was my roadie. He did not carry my guitar for me. Fun times.

The original Greezy Wheels at Willie's picnic in Bryan/College Station. Oh yeah, we knocked 'em out—you can tell by Sweet Mary's triumphant exit. If only getting paid had been that easy . . .

Photo by Sammy Mack Royal

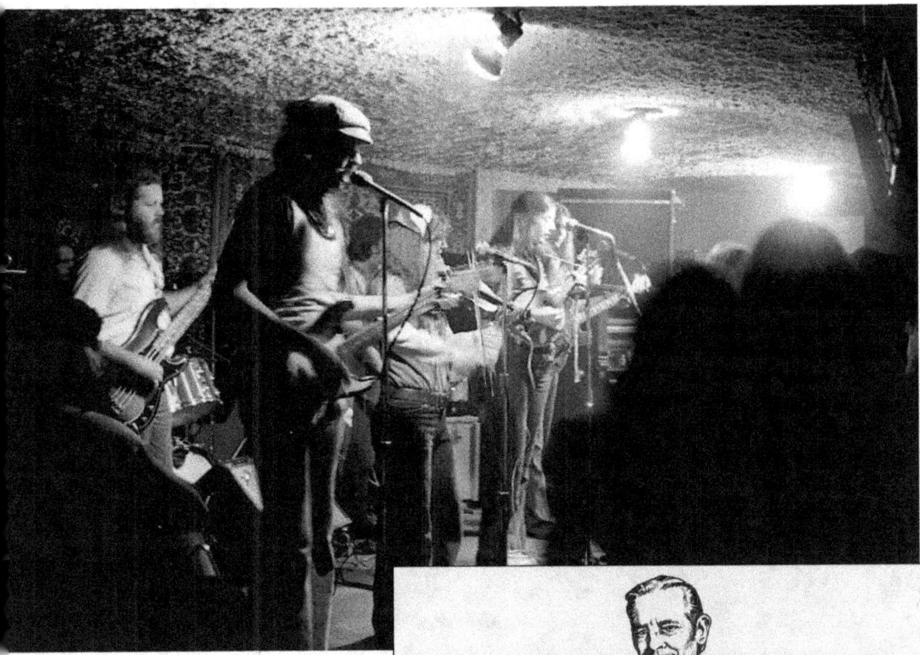

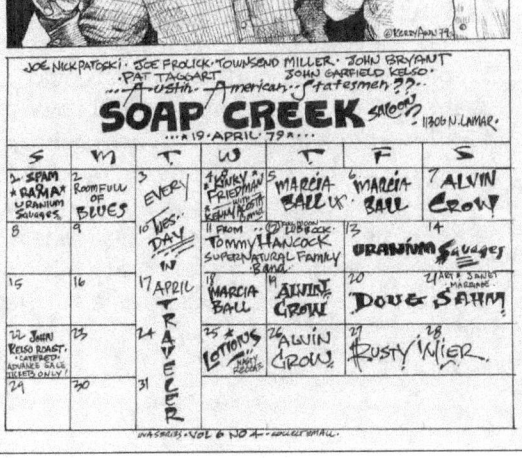

This is the Greezy Wheels on the Soap Creek Saloon stage, and one of the monthly calendars. That is me, in one of the ugliest hats ever. Check out the acts, folks. It'll give you an inkling how cool the place was. Note how Spamarama is spelled. This one likely featured one of the earliest spam toss events. If you'd like to get a glimpse of that stage on film, check out *Outlaw Blues,* with Peter Fonda and Susan Saint James. If you can find the original VHS, you'll see Lissa and Sweet Mary on the cover. Enter at your own risk. The poster drawing, by Kerry Awn, is of the amazing entertainment section staff of the *Austin American-Statesman*. They partied just as hard as we did.

Poster by Kerry Awn

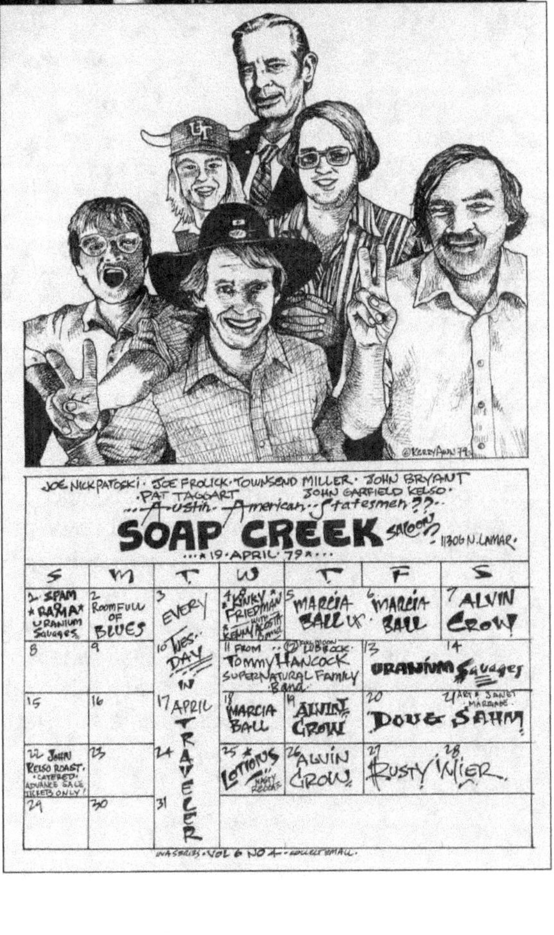

This giant hunk of womanhood is Rikke 'Big Rikke' Moursund, aka the Guacamole Queen. I cannot tell you how much the world misses her Aries presence. If you ever doubted or dared to ignore her always-amazing and accurate advice about your life and future, you got the full LBJ treatment. She towered over everyone except the giants among us, and you could not help yourself from saying, 'yes, ma'am, I will do this,' when she glared down at you. Whatever 'this' was, you did 'this.' These other guys are no slouches either. Behind Guac is David Arnsberger, co-founder of the legendary Austin band Uranium Savages—and the equally legendary ode to lunch meat, Spamarama. To the right, holding his son Ross, is George Majewski, co-founder of the greatest honky-tonk Austin ever had, the Soap Creek Saloon, the place that actually paid bands to come in and create mayhem. And mayhem we did create. I'm pretty sure the long, winding dirt driveway back to the road held the county record for driving off the road several years running.

Doug Kershaw, the very epitome of Crazy Cajun. Please note the position of my hands behind Doug. This was probably my best lick of the night. Here's a hint: If you're going to sit in with Doug, your fingers had better be mighty slick and awfully quick. Mine are none of that.

This was the show for which we received, like, a zero-star review, when, in fact, even Freddie admitted we toasted him pretty good. Rest in peace, while you can, Mr. Claypool. It won't be that long before I join you up there. Or down there, as it were.

Photo by Bruce Kessler/RockinHouston.com

Liberty Hall's Roberto Gonzales was famous for bringing in amazing bands for dirt prices. He was also famous for misspelling our names. There are still several posters in existence that feature 'Grezzy Wheels' as his headliner. He turned the broke-down Lido Theater in a broke-down part of Houston into a nexus for the best music ever presented in Houston. Broke-down Houston pretty much stayed broke-down for decades thereafter. Though we were never a country band, there was always a fair amount of cowboy hats in our audience. We figured it was our job to turn them on to the good shit.

Over the five years I managed the Lone Star Cafe, undoubtedly the most consistently exciting performer was Delbert McClinton. Everybody who was anybody came to see him, and most of them wanted to sit in with him. Always gracious, Delbert let them. They all wanted to be Delbert. Don't we all. Don't we all.

Photo by Carter Buschardt

Photo by Carter Buschardt

This guy never missed Delbert. Nor did he ever miss any of the coolest shows. He was Doc Pomus (seated here with Marshall Chapman). No matter how totally sold-out a show may have been, we managed to squeeze Doc and his wheelchair into his prime table. There, he would hold forth like Yoda on wheels, always with a story you'd never heard, always with several folks leaning in to hear him. When we had our first Lone Star Cafe reunion a few years ago at B. B. Kings in NYC, we held open a seat for Doc. Yep, the show was sold out . . .

You never knew who was going to show up on the Lone Star stage. Well, we knew Willie was going to show up every now and then, but pretty much everything beyond that was a surprise.

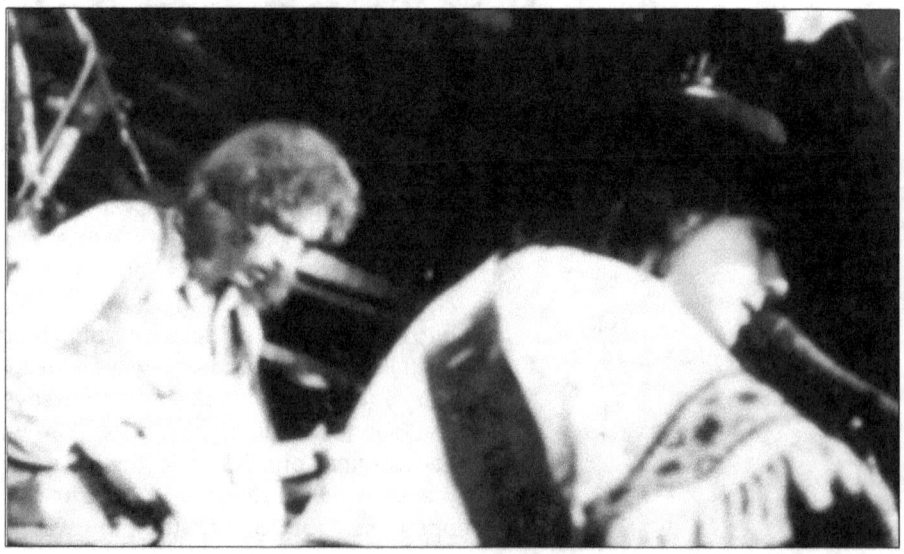

This is the best shot we could find of my sit-in with Lucinda Williams at the Lone Star. I wish I could tell you my performance was as cool as my haircut. It wasn't.

This is Robert Gordon at his most serene. A more normal shot would have him flailing his mike stand, snarling through clenched teeth, and dousing the front row with man sweat. With Tony Garnier on bass and guitarists like Danny Gatton, Chris Spedding, and Link Wray propelling him along, how could he not flail and sweat? Never a bad show for us at the Lone Star. Ever.

It took a while for me to get over my first payout to Albert King on his bus with his pistol in full view, but once we got to know each other (and he knew I was giving him a straight count at the door), we could chill together backstage. This is not my arm here, but my arm did often rest thusly on this big ole pussy cat. I miss him to this day.

Look at those soulful eyes, and you will understand what a sweet and humble man Bo Diddley really was. This shot was, of course, taken at the Lone Star Cafe. It's not a great shot, but one cannot miss the depth of this very old soul. The local bands he hired to back him for his Lone Star appearances adored working with him. I did too. The only thing complicated about Bo Diddley was the electronic package in his forty-pound, custom-made guitar. Bo stayed in great shape just lugging that monster to the stage.

I'm guessing this shot of Jaco is from early in the week. He rarely looked this together by week's end. Still, they were some of the most powerful shows I have ever seen. If only I had recorded even one of those nights . . .

This is the way Johnny always looked, like he was a man in a big-ass hurry. He was, and it cost him. His bandmates and pals followed him religiously at all times, mainly because stuff had a way of falling out of Johnny's hands and up their noses. . . .

Photo by Sammy Mack Royal

I like to call these the two sides of Kinky—pre-Cleve and post-Cleve. The pre-Cleve shot was taken at Willie's picnic in Bryan/College Station, TX. It's the same picnic featured in the photos of Greezy Wheels, but we had not yet met. I see absolutely no difference in the two Kinkys, except that he always wears dark hats now, and he no longer carries a man purse shaped like a peanut (or is that a pocked penis?). I'm betting he still has the flag poncho.

At Levon's Midnight Ramble with Sweet Mary and Lissa. Please note my blatant attempt at sainthood in my Baptist white ensemble. Nobody bought it.

The Ramble always closed with everyone joining in on 'The Weight.' Levon's on the drums. Sainted baritone's in the back. Mary was comping the horn section parts. The girl is a natural-born trumpet.

Moi Sweet Mary Pat Pankratz Mike Pugh Lissa Madrile Wilson Tony Airoldi Tony Laier
Melissa Pugh Cole Tracy Frederick (in the driver's seat)

Chip Dill Lissa Vic Egly Chris 'Whipper' Layton Sweet Mary Moi

Moi Sweet Mary John Jordan Lisa Pankratz David Roach Lissa Penny Jo (PJ) Pullus Randy Kirchhof Miguel Pankratz

Brad Houser Matt Hubbard Coleman Berg Moi/Sweet Mary Lissa PJ John (JB) Bush

JB Paul Mills Brad Airoldi Roach Mary Matt PJ Randy Lisa Miguel Madrile Tony Laier Vic Pat Lissa Mike Moi
John Jordan (behind Paul) (behind me)

These are the basic units of each generation of Greezy Wheels, from top to bottom. The very bottom photo is from our induction into the Austin Music Hall of Fame. We decided to all go in together. Super nerds will insist I name them all … so I will. Get out your looking glasses, nerds. Some are missing, some have passed on. None forgotten.

The real religion one got from attending church was good time, time taken off the end of your sentence for being a good little convict. Since I am an agnostic teetering on devil worship, you wouldn't think the church would be a good place for me. Surely either I or the church would burn in hell. But thirty days is thirty days, and you can compound the good time by being more devout than the rest of the innocents in your cell block and attending—religiously.

The problem being one must suffer the white Protestant view of religion. And the all-male white choir. So, basically, I didn't just join the choir because of my beliefs or to get my thirty days plus good time. I did it to upgrade the fucking choir. I may have a silky white coating, but I am a hundred percent silky black baritone at my center. Our stepmother had been named the White Priestess at an all-black church in Harlem. I coveted that honor. Yes, I am black and a bit of a princess as well.

The one redeeming member of the choir was the organist, a black jazz musician from Dallas who had big-time chops. After each rehearsal, I made him get down with whatever great riff he had in mind that day. After I sang something with him one afternoon, he encouraged me to do a solo the next Sunday. The minister, also a convict, had concerns, but he okayed me singing "May the Circle Be Unbroken," accompanying myself on guitar. I think he feared I was a Baptist bible-thumper. One could seek religion in the joint, but one did not thump. Thumping disturbed the populace.

The warden actually attended my performance that following Sunday. Word gets out when there's a star coming to town. After a totally non-stirring group performance of "He Walks With Me," I picked up the guitar, moved in front of the pulpit, and began to wail. I did not earn the nickname "Reverend Cleve" for nothing: By the second verse the entire congregation, except the warden, was dancing in their seats and singing along. To call it rousing would be weak. It was incendiary. Incendiary was another one of those little things the warden did not like. Along with thumping. Okay, yes, I was thumping. That's how I keep the beat.

Later that afternoon, I was summoned to the warden's office, where he told me that under no circumstances should I ever do that again in his church. Rather than dispute the ownership of the church—wasn't it the house of the Lord after all?—I apologized. For what, I'm not exactly sure. I did have one question. Was the warden afraid of the religious fervor of Protestants? A question not asked.

I gave up my thirty days' good time and quit the choir. That warden is the same guy who asked me to front the rodeo band. For which I got thirty days of good time. Religion be very strange inside the Walls.

I have met a lot of the heroes of my youth, but does this mean I'm special?

I don't mean gifted special, because that I am not. I'd have to be classified closer to special needs than specially gifted. You know, annoying in an almost Tourette-ish way. But some sort of special sauce must have come into my life to have, first, lived this fucking long, and, second, seen so much. I didn't just worship heroes from afar, I worshipped at their feet. In my own way, of course. My take on worship is to be smarmy and effete. I'm sure all my heroes loved me for that.

My first hero meet-up came at the age of thirteen. Mom had taken the family to NYC to meet Dad, who was sailing back from a year teaching at Oxford. They were already divorced, but Mom saw a chance to hit the Big Apple and took it. We had a big room at an old hotel on Broadway just above Times Square. The famous smoke ring–blowing billboard was right across the street. We had hadj-ed to the dead-ass center of American culture. I bowed to the Sabrett's Hot Dog vendors, newest members of my personal pantheon.

On our first night in, Mom wanted to go down the street to the Cafe Metropole to see Gene Krupa. Though it was I who truly appreciated his skills, and Mom was merely gaga over his cute puss and the glorious little curl of hair that wandered down his forehead whenever he soloed, I was to be left with bro and sis in the room. Until she was told single women were not allowed in unaccompanied—but that I could be her escort. Oh yay, Mom's escort . . .

Mom was a total hottie and plenty of trouble, exactly the kind of person the Metropole had in mind when they created their no-escort rule. I knew we'd get good treatment, but she was my mother for shit sake. How the fuck was I to rep my cool hanging with my spawner? After all, my voice was changing nicely, I had just begun my journey from chubster to lankster, and I had sprouted several pubic hair.

When we got to the Metropole and were seated in the back of the club, Mom discovered her wallet was missing, possibly stolen. After creating a huge hubbub, we tore back to the hotel where we found the wallet on the dresser. Upon our return, the hostess, who had witnessed our entire the-big-city-has-fucked-us episode, seated us right in front of Krupa this time. Eat that, Bob Uecker.

Gene was one of the two or three greatest drummers of his time, and he gave it good that night. I gave good audience in return. After the set, he came out in front of the drums and shook my hand, signed a photo for me. He was even friendlier with Mom. Turned out he was a somewhat touchy feely sort. S'okay by me—I had a cherished autograph of a true hero. Mom had an invitation to come back solo for the second show. I told you she was trouble.

I have no idea when Mom returned to the room that night, having long since crashed in a delirium of jazz drums and giant smoke rings. The next morning came fast, though, when we were awakened to hear Dad's boat was arriving four days late. This meant we were suddenly having to figure out a way to leave me in NYC to meet him so Mom could return home. It also meant we very quickly had to move on from the Metropole. All good. I had my memory, and you have this little story. One odd thing: I didn't have my picture. I never saw that autographed photo again. I'm betting big Mom swiped it. It was an action shot—it clearly displayed his glorious curl.

Working in dives like the Lone Star Cafe, it's almost impossible to not run across a hero every now and then. We booked a bunch of them in regularly, and since I worked four and five nights a week, metrics pretty much confirm this. I love metrics, though I'm not exactly sure how they work or even what some of them are. For example, what the fuck is WHIP in baseball? In this case, I not only do not know; I do not care.

Meeting James Brown would be a highlight in anyone's life. Trust me on this: Even if you had had no idea who he was, you would have been blown away by meeting him. He was just that sparkle plenty. He was one of those guys who wasn't just the center of the room, when he walked in; he *was* The Room. Screw metrics, James was about magnetics.

Booking the hardest-working man in show business was a major coup for us, something we'd dared not believe possible. But we just happened to ask him when he needed us. His career had sagged a bit, and he needed to make some noise in New York City. We were pretty sure he would do that, even in our little club, capacity 212. James Brown knew how to make noise. We knew how to blow up shit in the media.

We woke up terrified the morning of the show because the city's worst snowstorm in twenty years had passed through during the night. There was a good four to five feet of snow on everything, and nothing had been plowed or dug out. I was sure nobody would be able to make it, and we were going to tank. I barely made it in from Brooklyn Heights, myself, having left my snowshoes somewhere in fucking Fantasyland.

Astonishingly, we sold out both shows (and then some—*shhh*, don't tell the fire department), and the night went forth. Check that, it exploded forth. James used every inch of the newly expanded (by about three feet) stage; the band, whom we'd served a few extra shots of warmth, just destroyed the place; and at the end James collapsed beneath his cape three full times before finally being led downstairs by his soon-to-be manager Al Sharpton. Right, the Reverend, at that time one of the few people on the planet who could match James pompadour for pompadour.

It was in the dank super-heated basement that I got to hang with James Brown, whose full-on salon hair dryer was set up in the one well-air-conditioned office. James demurred on using the office, instead preferring to move the dryer into the middle of the hot dank. James liked it hot, on or off stage. It was surface of the sun under that dome, but the hottest air came from Sharpton, who whispered shit at him in a constant stream. I liked ole Al, except that he never shut up . . . about anything. That is still true . . . about anything. James mostly let his smile be his commentary. It said everything.

Beyond a shadow, my greatest childhood hero was Mickey Mantle. Besides having been born on my birthday, he played for my favorite team, the Yankees. They were my favorite team because they always won shit. I follow the frontrunners. Losers just . . . lose. You should probably note here that I am also a fair-weather friend. Win shit, we tight. Lose shit, who the fuck are you? It's the American way.

I must have had two dozen of those Mantle baseball cards as a kid. The problem with baseball cards though is that they are a perfect thickness to be the ammunition in rubber-band wars. Sling them correctly, and you could open a paper cut on the enemy, in my case either Ronnie Kern or David Kemp. A rubber-band war could last for hours. Every time we exhausted the armory, we'd gather up all the cards shot at us and sling those back across the battlefield. This, of course, is not the method for preserving memorabilia preferred by card fanatics. I reckon re-arming with the same cards today would cost several thousand dollars. I clearly lost that war.

So, when I finally met Mickey, I had nothing for him to autograph except maybe a Lone Star Cafe cocktail napkin, for that's where I got the chance to meet my greatest childhood hero. Of course—in a bar. Appropriate, since Mick was absolutely schnockered when we met. Billy (Martin, if you haven't been paying attention) brought him in one late afternoon along with two of the blowziest blondes I'd met to that date. I've met plenty o' blowzy babes since then, but these two stand at the top of the blowzy heap.

When they wobbled into the revolving door (and Mick had to rotate through the door twice, before finding his way in), I could tell it might be best to take them upstairs to the closed-off area. None of them were in any condition to deal with the public. On the way up, Billy introduced me to the babes, then to the Mick. Up to that moment, I had been in a state of awed denial—awed in his presence, in denial over the ass breath he belched into my personal space. That mouth had seen some horrible things.

He did slap me on the back and tell me, "any friend of Billy's, blah blah blah," before reeling up the stairs behind one of the blondes. He followed just closely enough to her that his face was bumper-to-bumper with her butt. He turned and leered at me, before he tripped and face-planted into that butt. He flashed a second leer before they disappeared into the dark front corner of the club. Mickey's drunken leer haunts me to this day. Cheshire cat meets Foster Brooks. Shudder.

They weren't there for more than fifteen minutes before I heard Billy yelling at Mickey. I nearly ran into him as he stormed out of the club. I had no idea what they were rumpus-ing over, my only bit of information being the last words heard from Mickey on my meeting with my greatest childhood hero: "Fuck him, girls. Let's go party." Some meetings just don't go as you'd expect them. However, does meeting childhood heroes make one special? You bet your ass it does.

Politics is for schmucks: You may call me Mister Schmuck

I'm not at all sure what made me say I wanted in on Kinky's gubernatorial run in 2006. I had always figured my role was to present my viewpoints from the stage, which can be a great bully pulpit. The trouble is that I've never had quite enough schmucks in my audience to do any damage. When given the opportunity to launch and caretake Kinky's campaign until his two professional hires from Minnesota could get to Texas and take over, I took it. In return for contributing ideas to Kinky's platform and receiving a nice paycheck, I entered the Schmuck Kingdom. I pretty much launched myself, dick first, into it.

It didn't matter that Kinky and I are polar in our politics. I had a strong hunch that his candidacy as an Independent was viable in a state that has a fairly equal number of Democrats and Republicans, but also has an overwhelming majority of dumb fucks and shitheads. I recognized that Kinky, with his decidedly fuck-you attitude, appealed universally to dumb fucks and shitheads. His appeal crossed the political divide. From leftist shitheads to rightist dumb fucks, everyone seemed to like the Kinkster.

My assignment was to make a BIG FUCKING DEAL of his launch, even though it was premature: We had no staff, no headquarters, and no real money had been raised. He could have waited until Dean Barkley and Bill Hillsman, his hired studs, came down mid-summer, but the Kinkster has never been one to have much patience with things. As soon as word got out that a formal announcement was coming, my home office phone went psycho. Me too. Kinky was already there.

I was definitely not thrilled to find messages from such as Bill O'Reilly piling up into the hundreds, but it did mean there was plenty of interest in a Jew musician running for Texas governor. Especially a gnarly, unfiltered, opinionated Jew from Kerrville. The media would eat him up for the next several months. Kinky would feast on the media as well. As we know, Kinky has always loved every conversation that revolved around himself. We even received several requests from Alex Jones, who latched on to the subversive-Jew angle. Evidently, Kinky was deep state. He's always been deep something.

We opted to launch the campaign from in front of the Alamo, with a second camera set-up inside the Menger Hotel across the street. The announcement would come on the Don Imus show. This was pre-nappy Imus, who still ruled the waves on MSNBC, and the audience was huge. If they'd all lived in Texas, Kinky would be in a third or fourth term as governor. That he's not is probably a good thing. If he were, I'd likely be the shoeshine guy at the mansion. That's what happens to former campaign managers. We devolve.

To spice up Kinky's grand entrance into Schmuck Kingdom, we were able to get seventy or so of Sweet Mary's fiddle students to dress up cowboy or Tex-Mex and bring their fiddles to San Antonio. They lined the staircase in the Menger atrium behind Kinky, when he came in from the shoot site in front of the Alamo, and played "Yellow Rose of Texas" before the official announcement. Which I didn't actually see. I had been going and blowing for weeks to prep this madness, and by the day of the show, my hemorrhoids had become murderous. I had retreated to our provided room to a fetal position and serial thumb-sucking.

The messages tripled on my machine overnight. It had worked. Kinky had made the big stage. I now had to guide him through the next three months until the cavalry arrived. I rented a small office on Congress Avenue that was immediately abandoned when John McCall, Kinky's largest contributor, offered up a huge warehouse/office on the south side of Austin. Please forgive John for investing a couple million in Kinky. He is neither a shithead nor a dumb fuck. He's merely a very good friend who thought it'd be cool to have his buddy in the state house. We all imagine that to be cool—until it actually happens.

Though I persevered mightily, and we managed to get Kinky to twenty-one points in the polls in a four-person race, the 'rrhoids never left the building all summer. I was delighted to hand over the reins to Barkley, the new campaign manager, and Hillsman, who would be the media weasel. Dean and Bill had been the guys who got Jesse Ventura elected governor of Minnesota as an Independent candidate. They had been deemed the "pre-eminent experts" on Independent campaigns. Unfortunately, independence in Minnesota and Texas means two different things. In Minnesota, it meant a former wrestler could attain the highest office. In Texas, it didn't mean shit.

Though Kinky had been the first candidate in Texas history to make it on the ballot as an Independent—all with strictly volunteer help—another candidate had bought her way on as an Independent as well. This kind of turned the tale from a maverick bucking the schmuck politicos to four schmucks on a ballot.

I began traveling to the Valley looking for support, while Team Minnesota started their work. In Barkley's case that mostly meant chewing on Kinky's expensive cigars in his office watching TV and fending off a serious case of gout. Hillsman created several cartoon ads that were clever enough I suppose, but ultimately he couldn't control his candidate, who started writing his own ad scripts. This is the last fucking thing you ever want to do in a campaign—let the candidate actually write his own copy. If Twitter hasn't taught you this by now, do yourself a favor: Never, ever enter politics.

The big play from the Minnesotans was to bring Jesse Ventura to Texas. The numbers had started sagging very soon after I left, and they figured Jess would ignite the populace. A successful media star and former governor supporting a media-star governor wannabe. It did seem like a good idea, but when Jesse arrived, his hair was halfway down his back and he sported a full-on Fu Manchu mustache/beard with fucking beads dangling from each end of it. Wrestlers and former governors may play well with Texas political schmucks, but long-haired hippies with fucking beads in their 'staches do not. Hippies with beads are more commonly used as targets in Texas.

Kinky ended up making several critical mistakes in his campaign, most importantly ignoring the black vote despite my having set up several meetings with key players—like Bobby Lee in Houston, who could have made a huge difference. Because he missed those meetings, he was attacked as being a racist, and he finished the race with about twelve percent of the vote. Now I know for a fact that Kinky is not a racist. For a child chess-prodigy genius, he's sometimes just unaware. Like everyone else. I forgive him for that.

And this is why I dove, dick first, into politics again, several years later. Again, it was a Kinky campaign. Have I mentioned that I am a bit of a self-flagellator?

"The road goes on forever, the party never ends"

Okay, if I'm still smoothing my funky old man dance moves post mortem, I might buy this, but my days on the road ended when I walked out of the Improv in LA in the middle of Kinky's two weeks of sold-out shows there and hightailed it back to Austin. One can only deal with so many hard miles, beer joints that wreak of puke, and stained hotel sheets that also wreak of puke before one finds oneself pondering a leap off the balcony of the fleabag provided by the club. Except that it's only two stories, a broken ankle at best. Not nearly good enough.

After performing and/or witnessing uncountable gigs good and bad, which puke-y joint was which gets lost. My theory is that as we age and we begin to have too many memories, we overfill our storage capacity and earlier memories are ejected out our assholes. Most of us have only four or five gigs of memory, and a life of over sixty years requires eight. Our brains reach critical mass and start losing shit. This shit flies out the asshole with the other shit.

The truly remarkable gigs do stay with you, each in a never-erase file that requires a password to open. For example, mention the password "The Other End" to me, and nearly every detail of our first Greezy Wheels shows in NYC flashes across my forehead. Yes, I have a movie screen set up on the inside of my forehead. For good memories, I just roll my eyes back into my skull and watch.

The Other End booking was our first for the powers that were at London Records. Or at least I recall it as that—two of the reels for this memory may have been switched—but I do remember a couple of the company weasels making us change places on stage for our second show, because they... fuck, there's one lost reel too. I have no idea why they wanted us to move. I just remember we hated it and switched back for the next show. With animus. We were from Texas. We didn't take to people pushing us around.

We were co-billed with Ronee Blakley, who was riding the rave over her appearance in "Nashville." It was an odd pairing. Ronee's act is a sort of high-brow chanteuse songbook mixed with just a sprig of good ole country gal. Greezy Wheels "fell between the stools" according to Rolling Stone, but mostly we jammed long and loud through high-tech, single-speaker Twin Reverb amps. Our shit could get loud.

The shows were well-received, both ours and Ronee's, but I remember little about the performances themselves. I do recall Mick Ronson sitting in with Ronee, mainly because he had to ask me to help him turn on my Twin, which I had let him use. Hilarious. Dude couldn't turn on the absolute standard of American rock amps. Best guess: British amps are driven on the right side.

It was the audience that made this gig. Kinky always

says a genius audience makes for a genius performance. I'm not sure I agree. I have sucked in front of many a genius and killed it in front of many a moron. Luckily, we kicked ass on the second show (back in our proper places on stage) in front of genius, an audience that included Kurt Vonnegut, Truman Capote and . . . David Cassidy. I'm pretty sure they came for the songbook, but we all hung out together at the end of the show until club owner Paul Colby kicked us out.

The conversation itself was a sort of extended jam, with a couple great writers and several decent songwriters all spouting witticisms and *mots*. You know you are in genius territory, when you get to witticisms and mots. Not many morons can spell either one. I can spell the shit out of mots. Cassidy remained mostly quiet, with an occasional half-hearted preen when one of the hot waitresses walked past. I can dig it. We males don't always have a full preen in us.

So it was a round-table moment. Of sorts. There was a bit too much gushing from the not-so-famous among us—mainly my sis, who asked for and received a personalized autograph from Vonnegut. But it did have just a taste of Algonquin Hotel to it, and the memory is still fresh and strong, albeit with a few reel problems. What is not still with us is that autograph, which Lissa cherished and lost almost immediately. Sigh, good thing we still have our inner foreheads.

I have always taken pride in being prepared for performance, but nothing can properly prepare you for doing a first gig in public after having spent a year in prison. When you are away

Life Is a Butt Dial 109

that long, the real world is put on hold. While inside, you are dealing with such basic daily routines, emotions, and survivals that when you re-enter life, information is suddenly coming at you too fast to process. Like the final scenes of "2001: A Space Odyssey," in which colorful shit is flying at you at hyper speed from all sides. Only it's not colorful shit. It's your fucking life.

I had expected to take a few weeks off to adjust to the free world, which we inmates simply called "world," but the Wheels had a date five days after my release. And there was no way I was going to be allowed to miss it, though I did protest. It was a weak protest to be sure. I was dying to see what the band had been up to while I was away. I probably should have protested a bit more forcefully. They had galloped ahead of me musically. Lissa, Mary, Mike, Pat, and Tony Laier had stayed together, and they had added Madrile Wilson on congas and Tony Airoldi, who had sat in with us on banjo previously, on guitar. Out of the gate, they were playing stuff much more sophisticated than anything we had done before. I was three lengths behind them before the first turn.

I had maxed out my musical growth on "Stagger Lee" with the prison band. I had no idea what my mates were doing. I could not process it fast enough. We were able to muscle-memory our way through several of the songs I sang, then I watched agape as they played several new ones. It was a successful homecoming, all in all. Except that I was still processing the first notes of the first tune long past the third encore.

Adding to my confusion was the opening act, Billy Joe Shaver. His show didn't confuse me at all. His songs, every one of which became a classic, were right up a convict's alley. His lyrics and his personality are one and the same, and his heart is right there on that rolled-up dungaree shirtsleeve. Of course, one must be aware there might also be a small-caliber pistol up that sleeve.

The confusion was in my inability to discern between Billy Joe and Darrell Royal, who was also at that show. We had come to know Darrell, the coach of the Texas Longhorn football team, through his kids, who were fans and friends of the Greezy Wheels. But I was so out of it that night (remember: still processing those first notes), I could not tell the difference between Darrell and Billy Joe.

They both did have that same sharp-cheeked Okie handsomeness that only sharp-cheeked Okies and Billy Joe Shaver have. Rugged was written into their jaws. Each time I stood in front of them, I felt like a strobe light was interfering with my thoughts—the forehead screen was blank—and I could not tell them apart. Unless I shook their hands. You always know it's Billy Joe when you encounter the finger deficit. He's missing two on his right hand. Quick subtraction reveals the truth.

I'm sure both BJ and Darrell were a bit perplexed that each time I encountered them backstage, I shook their hand. Which I did at least three times each. I am one friendly motherfucker.

All musicians are artistes—some are actual artists

In my view, most artistes have no discernible talent other than a sense for drama and an innate desire to do cabaret. This differs from the artist, the one genetically inspired to find the fucking musical answer, no matter the hardship, no matter the shithole blues joint. However the real artists, the ones with actual genius, are often artistes, as well. This is because neither the artist nor the artiste is a normal person. Both of these subgroups of Homo sapiens do really weird shit, very often to the point of being Homo annoyance.

It's as if one must have quirks if one is to be or pose as an artist. Most of the quirky ones I have encountered have been real artists—I placed myself in the middle of that highway to not miss them—so they are forgiven for their idiosyncrasies. They are charming little faults in otherwise "perfect" people. The quirks of the artistes, not so charming. I've often fantasized target practice at local musical productions, having had to deal with the artiste directors and Robert Goulet wannabes or soap stars who think they have a second career as a singer-songwriter.

Whether it's major quirks or minor ones, they will get under your skin, even when it's the true artists. Eric Andersen is a true artist and a minor case in point. Eric is chock full of quirks that leave him constantly antsy, always moving on to something else before you've finished where you just were, never quite comfy in his own skin. And I love the guy, strange and off-putting as he is at times. But I absolutely hated paying him after a performance at the Lone Star.

When it's time to pay the headliner, it's time to get the fuck outta Dodge. Other than comparing notes with the bartenders or flirting with the half-lit waitresses as they sneak liquor or food out the back door, your last important duty of the day is pay the star, leave. Most folks or their reps know this, and they are adept at taking a wad of bills and counting them without the wad leaving their hands. One count, straight through the pile. All managers appreciate this kindness.

Eric may not have known this—he is kind of extra-dimensional in his unawareness. Eric always insisted in laying out his bills in individual piles of a hundred bucks each. If it was a hundred-dollar bill, it got its own pile. Instead of counting the piles immediately, he then went through each pile and turned every bill in the same direction *before* counting the money. Which was always right: never more, never less than what he was supposed to get. Except the slap across the side of the head I was supposed to give him in that extra dimension.

Some of the quirks of the true artists come from the hard roads they travel. They have seen so many variations on the basic theme of *play the gig, find the manager, get the money, verify the money, leave town without being killed,* that they develop mental and procedural systems to deal with any and all situations. Albert King had a basic no-nonsense way of doing his biz, and if you didn't do it right, he didn't play the gig or never came back. This is actually shit I well understand.

To get Albert into the Lone Star, we had to practically re-route traffic on Thirteenth Street and Fifth Avenue to ensure he had a space for his bus—the bus that only he drove. No bus? Albert's moving on. On at least one occasion I paid a Lone Star porter to stand for two hours in Albert's space until Albert arrived. This may have put the porter's life at risk—New Yorkers will literally kill for a parking space—but it was worth it for the performance that he always gave.

And whereas Eric Anderson's payout scenario was quirky, Albert's was scary quirky, at least the first time I had to pay him. At the end of his show, he told me to pay him on the bus about a half-hour afterwards. He first had to collect fifty bucks from two of his sidemen for the single error each made in the set. Yikes. Albert did not fuck around. I wasn't sure I wanted to step onto the bus at all. Surely a blues legend wouldn't shoot me and drive away with my body if there was a miscount. Would he?

As I entered the bus, this question loomed even larger when I saw that there was nothing inside that bus except one chair all the way in the back. With one giant black man planted in it. Albert was a very large man. The only other item I could see on the entire bus was a pistol resting at Albert's side.

I nearly bolted, but Albert had me sit on the wheel well

opposite him and hand him the money. I nearly knelt in front of him in obeisance as I handed over the thrice-counted dough. He counted it in about four seconds—it never left his hand—and smiled his approval. I started to gush that gush of relief one gushes when you figure out you are going to survive a near-death experience, but Albert told me to leave, that he had to "move on to Boston." Which was okay. I had to move on to the men's room before I crapped myself.

Beyond a doubt, the quirkiest performer with whom I ever shared a stage is Willis Alan Ramsey. Other than myself of course. Hey, after all these years hanging with quirks and flat-out loonies, I deserve a little slack if I'm a little . . . odd. Or extremely odd. But Willis tops the bill outside my skin. Upon seeing him for the first time, I had no clue of his weirdness. I was pretty sure of my own.

One of Willis's earliest (if not his first) shows in Austin occurred in front of us at the long-gone, somehow-legendary-but-never-as-beautiful-as-all-that Hungry Horse. One of Greezy Wheels' first regular club gigs, the Hungry Horse was a beer and set-ups bar. It became all about Lone Star beer quite quickly in our reign at the Horse, as one of our most well-received tunes was Pat Pankratz's classic "Country Music and Friends," which included the line "cocaine, country music, and good ole Lone Star beer." The owner, Mike, had to order ever-greater quantities of Lone Star to soothe the savages. The brewery fucking loved us.

The club was all about the beer; we were all about the blow. Not that we could afford to actually have any blow. Nobody was supplying ever-greater quantities of that.

We often had other performers asking if they could do

an opening set for us. More often than not, those openers sucked. The Austin music scene still had a ways to go. I actually asked around for a shepherd's-crook supplier more than once. Have you ever tried to drag someone off stage who had no idea they were gawd-awful and insisted on doing a full set? Of gawd awful? Shepherd's crook—works every time.

So it was that one evening Willis Alan Ramsey asked if he could do a few songs. Willis was a little better kept than most of the folks who opened for us, and he seemed a whole lot more confident. He knew how to adjust a mic stand. A sign of a pro. As it turned out, he also knew how to play. Really knew. It was our first true dusting by an opening act. His songs were killer, his performance captivating, his smile winning. I found myself hating to admit the guy was the *package.* He had it all. I wanted to be the package. I'd have died for the winning smile.

I couldn't believe myself when I told him he could play with us anytime. I wanted to say: "Your mother's calling you, kid. Go home." That fucking winning smile.

The last show we did with Willis was a women's rights fundraiser at some long-forgotten joint on Sixth Street hosted by Sarah Weddington. There was something different about Willis. He still had his winning smile (much chagrin here), the great tunes, the fine-tuned performance . . . except that the performance was more performance interruptus than performance perfectus. It seemed that his environment had become his enemy. Every time a register rang out, he stopped playing—usually mid-song—to admonish the poor bartender for just doing what she was being paid peanuts to do: sell shit to keep the dive alive.

In fact, he stopped for *every* noise, including a sneeze. Now, I have stopped shows in my life for a medical emergency, for an important announcement from the venue, and to beat the crap out of a particularly annoying heckler. I have never stopped one for a sneeze. Something was brewing inside that perfectly formed head of Willis Alan Ramsey. It looked to be about a keg of insanity.

His music had started making him a ton of money, most notably of course "Muskrat Love," which a little-known hard-rock duo with a captain's hat took to number one on the charts. And Willis disappeared, possibly behind that pile of money. My understanding is he made somewhere around four million bucks for that song alone. He has never released another album. Since 1972.

You cannot tell me he lost his talent. You don't lose talent. However, you can lose *touch* with your talent. I did so for twenty-three years when I put Greezy Wheels in retirement (that thankfully turned into a hiatus), thinking I could stay in touch with my talent by managing clubs and other entertainers. Sadly, you don't manage others with talent. You do it with whips and chairs, somewhat like handling circus animals.

We have heard many times over the years that Willis was finally getting ready to put out a new record, then . . . nothing. My theory is, yes, the money did it. It drove him into insanity. And it has kept him there, via the continuing royalty checks. Naturally, I would like to test that theory. All I need is forty-six more years and four million bucks.

Nothing is more fun for a writer than having your own column

I take that back. Getting *paid* for having your own column is more fun, but as writing gigs go, columns are the shit. Especially when your editor doesn't give two shits what's in your column as long as it meets deadline. Meeting deadline is my best subject. Regardless of the drivel I hand in, my work comes in a nice tidy folder with impeccable indentations and terrific fonts. My editor literally did not care if my column was dog shit. It often was. But that shit was on fucking time.

My column happened to be in *OUI* magazine, a men's "journal" founded by Hugh Hefner but later sold to a guy who couldn't spell journal. By the time I arrived at *OUI*, there were as many cock shots as spread shots, and most of the spreads and cocks were engaged. Right, pure porno. My biggest ongoing fight was not about content. It was about refusing to allow my column to be placed opposite a full-page photograph of a ten-inch penis.

My column was called "The Idiot and the Odyssey," which pretty much spoke to its content. I was an idiot on a *hejira* to the blank spots in America, the places in between reality and my life. That is quite a lot of blank. Reality and I are not close. We acknowledge each other, cross paths occasionally, and sometimes admit to each other's existence.

I took on the tough assignments, like finding the best cheeseburger amongst the "upscale" chain joints like Hard Rock Cafe, Planet Hollywood, and the Motown Cafe. The latter two are no longer with us (and trust me: *nobody* misses them). This can be partially blamed on the horrendous cuisine, but mostly they failed because the only people who worked there were under the sadly mistaken notion they might be discovered by the restaurant owners, like Bruce Willis or Berry Gordy. Actors make terrible waiters. Forget fucking musicians.

And do not fool yourself into thinking you're going to eat great food at Hard Rock Cafe just because it still exists. The Hard Rock is all about memorabilia, not memorable grub. Unless you have a fondness for Rick Derringer's guitar picks as appetizers. Needless to say, I found no good food at any one of these joints. Nor any reason for any of them to exist.

My only real try for a truly newsworthy column was my attempt to join the Church of Scientology in Los Angeles. For one day. You know, to find out first hand why suckers are sucked into this pit of religious misery. My foray into the world of e-meters and Tom Cruise lasted about ten minutes, when I tried to take a few photos of the original church on Hollywood Boulevard. (I took all my own photos for my column.) As soon as I snapped picture one, two very scary-looking trolls oozed out of the front door and took down my license number. I thanked them for being scary trolls and bolted to the Roosevelt Hotel, never to return. Hello heebie-jeebies.

There is a surprise in every box of Cracker Jacks: I found an even better story sitting in the Cinegrill, the famed club that once sat inside the lobby of the Roosevelt. On stage that night was one of my favorite all-time comedians, Pat Paulsen, who was doing a double bill with Murray Langston (the Unknown Comic). I had met Murray through Ruth Buzzi, Kinky's longtime friend. He's a great guy who probably did one too many Gong Show appearances to sustain a long-term high-profile career.

I had also befriended Ruthie and her husband Kent after meeting them at a Kinky show in LA. My first impression of Ruthie was her ass, which was nestled in between Kent's legs and pointed directly at the stage for most of Kinky's set that evening. She and Kent were a relatively new couple at that time. They were forgiven for acting like teenagers on Make Out Hill. I can never forgive that this impression remains in memory. Gotta admit though: Ruthie had a great ass.

Murray quickly introduced me to Pat and hit the stage for his show. As soon as I mentioned Ruthie's name to Pat, he was my pal. We proceeded to talk through Murray's entire set, which may or may not have bothered Murray. It's possible the bags not only hid his face, but also blocked out the world. I've often considered bagging my head to achieve the latter.

It turned out Pat had a real agenda, had he been elected president. We never discussed that agenda, but I do believe he was at least half-serious about politics. He knew there was more money to be made as a corrupt politician than as an honest comic; therefore winning something was his little daydream. His show was a stopper—I laughed so hard my heart nearly stopped beating—and we continued chatting afterwards until the bar closed. I'm writing him in for president in 2020. I don't care if he is dead. He'd still do a better job of it than any "serious" politician.

Not all of my adventures were quite as glorious. I searched for the Great Mouse at Disneyworld, learning only that most of the pretty young guides and ride operators also worked at Orlando's most popular topless club—and that my hatred of all amusement parks was justified. Sorry, kids. Uncle Cleve will just enjoy a bit of hara-kiri while you hit the tilt-a-whirl.

For another column, the biker convention in Daytona Beach was . . . interesting. I was desperate to find a great-looking woman to photograph as my Miss Daytona Beach pick for the story. None of the ladies I spoke to along the main drag were interested. Every single one asked if I was from *Playboy*. Every single one told me to fuck off when I said I was from *OUI*.

Here's a little tip about searching for your cover girl at a biker convention: Do not—I repeat, do not—look for her at a wet t-shirt contest on the outskirts. I'm sorry, ladies and gentlemen: Some people should never (I mean *ever*) show off a wet set in public. I'll keep the Ruthie memory. Please, Lord. Just let me lose this one.

I finally chose my landlady for that week as my Miss Daytona Beach. She had had one of the last available spaces to rent in Daytona, a spare bedroom I shared with her treasured shrine to Jesus. She was seventy years old. Perfect. I shot her astride one of the Harleys owned by another house pest. Take that, ten-inch-cock shot.

For one story, I looked for the soul of Las Vegas, finally finding it in Willie Nelson, who was playing at Orleans. Hanging backstage in a plush theater with Willie, Poodie, Bee, and the boys was fun and very soulful, but once they drove off to the next show, Las Vegas immediately reverted to its soulless self. Surprise, surprise.

I am nearly ashamed to say I went bow hunting for feral hogs in West Texas with Ted Nugent. This was in the mid-Nineties, before he was known for his asshole politics. He was simply known as an asshole. Ted was all about being a self-sufficient bad-ass he-man motherfucker. He was anti-pot, which fucked any chance of me liking him in the first place, and very proud that he had hair on his chest. He was not exactly pleased that I remembered his first appearance at the Fillmore East with the Amboy Dukes—and that he wore a darling little flowered jumpsuit for his debut. He couldn't have looked more effeminate if he'd worn lipstick.

I did learn one valuable lesson from this experience: how to kill a rattlesnake. You do it with a rock. I am rock expert. Ugh.

I am also now an expert on piercing a clitoris, which I not only witnessed but also photographed. The first thing every woman should know about this is that she should not do it. Really, I mean this. I still shiver a bit imagining my dick getting caught in a pussy ring. Please ladies, consider my concerns.

My volunteers for the piercing couldn't have been more than nineteen, and I'm guessing they hadn't thought things through vis-à-vis how this would work on a sexual basis. They knew the piercings would work on a performance basis—they both worked at a topless/bottomless joint—but did they stop to consider maybe that most men wouldn't want to be encountering anything hard in that area other than themselves? I think not.

As you can see from these few examples of my columns (I did it monthly for about two years), I am a very serious reporter. I cover the big stories. My paragraph indents are impeccable, my fonts are off the hook. And I have learned much about the human condition. I have learned that Ruth Buzzi has a great keister, Pat Paulsen would have been a rad president, and do not fuck with Scientology. Oh yeah, and rock beats snake.

What do you say to a giant dragonfly?

Apparently, you say yes. In 1982, Mort did just that when maxi-artist Bob "Daddy-O" Wade asked if we had a need for a giant dragonfly at the Lone Star. With that listed capacity of two hundred and twelve and weekend crowds that often reached a thousand sweaty, dancing-in-their-seats (and almost always obnoxious) people, sure, the club had plenty of room for a fucking twelve-by-sixteen-foot bug.

The critter, dubbed *Dragonfly Texanus Giganteus* and captured somewhere between Laredo and Bob Wade's frontal lobe, was so large, the only place for it inside the club was directly over and high above the postage-stamp stage. Bill Dick had the construction skills to hoist and position the hundred-and-fifty-pound sculpture, but the often-heard rumors of Bill's mob connections in Queens gave rise to some fears of faulty construction. That's a New York thing. *Capiche?*

But one giant dragonfly could easily have taken out a full band if held up by the wrong materials. Imagine if it had fallen on James Cotton or Etta James. Dragonflies would never have lived it down. Wade would be living in a dirt-floor shack somewhere in the third world. No, he'd likely have been crucified, which I believe is another of Bob's secret dreams (imagine the price of his work after a fucking crucifixion!). Fortunately, it did not come down until the gavel came down at auction at the closing of the Lone Star Cafe a few years later.

And so the dragonfly flew off to parts unknown, perhaps never to be seen again. Rumor has it the Big Bug landed a gig at a small, out-of-the-way tavern in Upstate New York, wherein the tavern owner has it rigged to drop down from above the bar at the push of a button. I'm thinking more than one drunk has shit his pants in a small, out-of-the-way tavern in Upstate New York.

Just remember: Every gig is as good as the last one

Really? Have you been listening to me or not? I thought not. All gigs are different, even shows in the same venue. On the whole, especially at the club-tour level, most pretty much suck. You don't notice this until well into your fifth or sixth year touring. You are so juiced with the idea that being on the road leads directly to fame and fortune that it never occurs to you that your life is also starting to suck. It's only after you've seen the same clubs a few dozen times, endured the individualized indignities they each provide, that you realize you have bamboozled yourself. You also come to the understanding that you might, in fact, be an idiot.

You begin to endure the not-quite-as-fun gigs and look forward longingly to the top-shelf joints. I'll put up with two shithole joints for one great theater show any day. After a while, you begin to see the karmic balance. You are supposed to eat shit on a regular basis to occasionally get cake. All I know is I've eaten a lot of shit, but it's been a while since I've had cake.

But I *have* had cake. When Greezy Wheels first signed with Agency for the Performing Arts, the first gig we got from them was at . . . a comedy club . . . in fucking Miami. For six days. We had never been to Miami and had never played one club six nights in a row. In that era, Miami was a place for little old Jewish couples migrating down from Queens, NY, not Texas ex-pats. Certainly not *hippie* Texas ex-pats. We were not happy. It seemed we had been swindled in life again.

Until we saw the marquee. We were co-billed with Steve Martin. From then on it didn't matter that we were fleabagged in the worst section of Miami, had almost no money, and were forced to eat every day at a hash house on the corner of Hooker and Pimp Street, a place that made a Waffle House look like Oz. None of this mattered. We were working with fucking Steve Martin.

We spent six nights in awe. I rarely spend six seconds in awe, given my effeteness, but we were watching a mind much better than we'd ever seen before at work. For two shows a night. We only left the room long enough between shows for the club to clear the house and the band to clear its minds. We tried to get Steve to join us on the bus for a smoke break, but upon seeing our puke-green '49 Flexible Flyer, he begged off. We understood. Steve was just about to explode into arenas and stadiums. He was on the verge of the chauffeured life. Messy band buses with exceedingly impolite toilets were no longer a part of his life . . . if they ever had been.

We watched every single performance, never stopped laughing, and marveled anew each night at his quickness on his feet. Steve watched every one of our shows, too. This pleased my ego no end until I realized a couple things: It occurred to me that he was actually trapped inside the venue. He hadn't hired his first limo yet, and where the fuck does one go between sets at a small comedy club anyway? The "green room" was a storage closet. I noticed, too, that he wasn't reacting all that well to us. My mood went polar. Suddenly it didn't matter that we were on tour in support of our first album on London Records, signed to a major agency, and hot shit in Austin. Steve hated us. Life sucked.

Or so I thought until the very last set of the week, a week in which we discovered Steve was a very serious, low-key guy off stage who wore black-silk underwear. For Steve's last set of the week, he did nothing but play the banjo. No comedy, just pickin'. He was just as fucking good on banjo as he was on arrows through the head, and he was sticking it to our nascent banjoist, Tony Airoldi. It turns out it had been Tony causing that look of bad-taste-in-the-mouth Steve had had all week watching us. Tony was not nearly as good on banjo as he was (and is) on guitar. Steve was the real-deal banjoist. He had made his banjo bones at Disneyland.

This meant I was still golden. He merely hated Tony's picking. It didn't matter that I didn't know if Steve liked me or not. It was just so much better than knowing he did not like me. I call that a tie in favor of the runner.

One of the most interesting shows the Greezy Wheels ever did was a wedding. We never asked specifically for wedding gigs, nor could anyone have ever confused us with a wedding band. Perish the fucking thought. But on this occasion, we, along with Willie, were asked to play for David Allan Coe's wedding—or at least one of them. David was an up-and-coming bad-ass guy at the time and one of the few musicians beside myself who had done deep prison time. I liked him for that, so we took the gig. Ex-cons be watching other ex-cons' backs. I had not yet figured out he was a piece of work ex-con. Some ex-cons change for the good, some just stay piece of work. David Allan Coe is *Mister* Piece of Work.

The wedding was held at Sons of Herman Hall in Dallas (if I recall correctly), and there was a full house. I'm pretty sure Coe charged a cover for the wedding. There's a concept I should have thought of for my children. Fuck that: Why didn't Mary and I do it? We were paid before our set, so I didn't really give a shit. Or even think about it. I was a low-concept thinker back then.

We did our set, Willie did his set, everybody got stinkin' ready, and finally it was time for the ceremony. Willie played preacher (prepping for a later movie role?), and somebody, probably Mickey Raphael, played the wedding march. I played with my belly button. On any other gig we'd have been packed up and on the road halfway through Willie's set, but I did want to stick around and get a look at the blushing bride, the Mrs. Piece of Work to be.

There was not much blush left to this bride. I suppose there might have been, but it's hard to see a blush against a black background. The bride wore all black. I was almost too busy trying to delve this symbolism to notice David's ensemble. There was no delving it. Coe was wearing giant old-style motorcycle goggles on his puss, black everything else, with a pair of giant leather balls swinging in front of his scrotum. I have to say it was declarative. Even in my higher-concept thinking, which kicked in about fifteen days ago, I still cannot delve the symbolism. I do wonder who kept the balls when they split up.

Best pure gig ever? I'd have to rate Levon Helm's Midnight Ramble as my fave. The barn in which he had them is three stories of redwood warmth that produced some of the finest sound ever heard outside a recording studio. It is, in fact, a recording studio and has been for a whole bunch of folks. But it was the warmth of Levon himself that made things so especially cool. It was as if he had taken everything that is good out of Arkansas and brought it to his little space in Woodstock. This, of course, left nothing good in Arkansas.

People paid very high ticket prices to see very special shows, and we were delighted to do two of them. The first one was the chart-topper, a triple bill of Levon and his ace band, Billy Bob Thornton, and us, with a short opener by Little Sammy Davis. Chris Robinson of Black Crowes horned in for a couple tunes, so there was a bit of *meh* mixed in with the yeah.

We conquered that night: John Jordan on bass, John Bush on drums, Penny Jo Pullus on Greezette, and myself, Mary, and sis Liss. We stormed the palace and were welcomed with open arms by the villagers. Larry Campbell joined us for a rousing fiddle finale, and we encored the village into adoring submission. Whether or not any musician will admit it, encores are not only a great feeling for you, they are wonderful little fuck you to the act that has to follow you. Not that we had any bad intentions toward Billy Bob, but fuck you, nonetheless.

Billy Bob's show was as strange and wondrous as Billy Bob himself. There were, like, four guitar players, they all had cool retro suits, and the lighting made them all ethereal. The ethereal thing can be partly attributed to the quality of the weed being passed around out back in the two large buses that served as green rooms. The whole evening was a foray into ethereality.

Billy Bob's music itself doesn't need drug intake to seem ethereal. It's kind of cosmic, kind of cowboy, slicker all the way. It reflected not only Billy Bob's character, but probably all the characters he had played in his films. Except Sling Blade. If anything, Billy Bob is the antithesis of Sling Blade. He exists somewhere between Switch Blade and Blade Runner. As does his music. And he has Angelina's blood in a fucking vial.

Every Ramble ended with all performers joining together on stage to sing along on "The Weight." I don't usually join in these types of singalongs, not having much of a harmony voice and all, but I did so with great glee with Levon. Mary was even more delighted: She got to sit in with the horn section, something she'd always wanted to do. You'd be amazed at how trumpet-y she plays the trumpet parts on her fiddle. You'd swear it was lips making those sounds, not a bow. Mary has world-class lips on the violin.

The custom at the Ramble was to join Levon in his kitchen adjacent to the barn for peace pipes and palaver after the show. We never pass up peace pipes, even if we've been passing them for several hours before the chief beckons. Palaver is our second-best subject. Once again, I had a Yankee-locker-room moment. Everyone at the table hollered "Cleve" as we entered. My ego can just never get enough of those locker-room moments. Eat it, id.

Before I could retrieve the pipe floating my way, Levon handed me a righteous bud and told me to stick it between my cheek and gums. I told Levon I'd much rather reload the pipe then inches from my reach, but he insisted. Damn, if he wasn't right. My gums immediately numbed, and my body readily accepted its THC content. I still glommed onto the pipe, mind you.

We sat around for about thirty minutes reminiscing, toking, laughing, toking, and it finally dawned on me exactly how hip Levon Helm was. Everyone at the table had a good level of hip, but Levon was the coolest. We'd all seen plenty in our time, could easily have talked for days about it, but Levon knew more, much more, than any of us. Bless his heart, Billy Bob is one hip guy, but he's a nebbish compared to Levon. Levon was the top cat. No doubt.

Recording studios are the shit

Granted, some are just shitty, but getting to be *in* a studio is always the shit. There is nothing like it for anyone driven by music and sound. If only I could have lived my entire life inside a recording studio. These days I kinda do, what with my crackerjack computer that constantly entertains me with the little whirling ball, my ancient Pro Tools app, and my single Rode K2 mic. Right, I live in a shitty studio.

When Greezy Wheels was offered a recording contract by London Records, the battle we chose over that contract was in demanding control of the music and the chance to record in great studios. How foolish are the young. We should have been battling over the bucks, because essentially we didn't get any. There was a small advance, but it was not a gift. When we were later dropped by the label in a corporate shakeup, they sent us a bill for fifty-seven grand. I countered with an invoice for fifty-seven grand. For personal services.

We got the studios, because everybody got great studios, but in those days full control of the product for a newbie band was simply not on the table. London proved it by completely remixing one of the tunes to their own tastes for the first single. That single was recorded in a Westlake Audio facility, which, I was told, was super fucking fragilistic, the top of the line in studios. I knew blank about Westlake Audio, but I did know about super fucking fragilistic, me being kind of a fragilistic guy myself. We agreed on the studio.

Unfortunately, the studio was not in NYC or LA. It was in the bowels of Louisiana—Bogalusa to be exact. Great, we were recording in a swamp. Okay, I do give it some credit: It was not in a swamp but the woods, and it was pretty as all get out. But there was something tragically swampy about the place. It was the stench of something unholy that hovered in the woods. An odor so evil it beckoned one to stick a sharp object up one's nostril. It was the smell of rotting brussels sprouts.

It came from a paper mill about a mile from the studio. Apparently all paper mills smell like rotting brussels sprouts. Adding insult to nostril injury was the daily menu choice of the cook provided us by the studio. And I think it was a conscious fuck-you to us hippie weirdos. Every evening for the week we were there, she served brussels sprouts. Can you feel your stomach turning yet?

The studio itself was nice—lots of wood and odd angles and shit—and the album we tracked there, our first, has its moments. But to this day, I cannot look a brussels sprout in its wrinkly little face. I carry sharp things with me at all times. I'm ready, in case one sneaks up on me.

The album must have sold just enough, because London let us do a second record. This time we got to go big time. We started tracking at Electric Ladyland, an absolute thrill for all of us. We were in the studio spawned for and by Hendrix. We sat at the same board, in the same room, on the same chairs, probably in the same blue haze of great pot smoke. It would have been perfect (and nearly was)—except for KISS.

KISS was working on their "Dressed to Kill" album in the adjacent studio, with a slightly different take on playback volume. Volume-wise, KISS is the living Spinal Tap. Their shit goes off at eleven on the volume knob. We would have to wait for them to either break or finish for the day to record anything, without getting the sound of KISS thunder through the supposedly perfectly soundproofed wall. This is another one of those things that has lingered with me ever since. I reach for my shotgun every time a boombox car drives by our house at full volume. Luckily for them and the world, I do not actually own a shotgun. Mary is no dummy.

I got into a philosophical yet still shallow conversation with Gene Simmons years later at the Lone Star Cafe when he came in with Diana Ross. KISS hadn't yet taken off the grease paint, so he went unrecognized. While she sat in the spotlight at the premier balcony table, Gene groused at the bar in the dark. I had recognized him from Ladyland, but nobody else did. My schadenfreude kicked in. Yep, I was still pissed over his excessive volume. And watching others grouse is a lifelong preoccupation.

Gene droned on about what brought him to rock-and-roll—that he had been a school teacher but discovered that he "reached more young people" with his music. I listened, I nodded my head in the correct moments, I posed well-practiced sympathetic facials, all the while thinking to myself, *See? If you had just turned down your fucking amp, it'd all be all right.*

We finished recording the tracks for that record at the

Record Plant in Sausalito, where my dream of living in a studio first blossomed. This is because at this time, Sly Stone *did* live at the studio. He'd had a special room built to his own specs, including a sound-board area that was sunk below the recording areas with only a one-foot glass window separating the two spaces. Less than ten feet away was a full bedroom with a full-sized bed. We didn't meet Sly, but I sneaked into the room to lie on his bed. And dream a little dream.

We did meet and hang a bit with Bill Wyman, a conversation begun after he had bumped into my sis, Lissa. Lissa is a tall person, and it turned out Bill is a quite short person. When they collided, his face smashed into her breast. I am sure Lissa continues to cherish the memory.

My very first recording experience ranks among the most unusual of all time, and I don't just mean in my life. I mean in the history of the galaxy (and I'm sure there have been some strange sessions in the outer worlds). My first chance to make a record came . . . in prison. And not just any prison. We tracked it at the Goree Unit of the Texas prison system, at that time the one women's prison in the state. Oh yeah, we rock stars were gonna take it down, strut our stuff amongst the pulchritude.

Of course, exhilaration begins when you're taken to the cage car and driven outside the walls. You cannot help but feel just a tad freer than you were that morning waiting in the commissary line, no matter that you are chained together. That we were going to a place chock full of women was double the excitement, especially for our lifer rhythm section, neither of whom still had family to visit them, both of whom had begun to concern me over their long meaningful looks at each other.

Our nervous chatter reached a peak just as we pulled up to the front entrance. It de-escalated into a downhill slalom when we were told our first task. For some reason, the warden had decided to send a B-3 organ ahead of us, although we had never used one in our shows. The sergeant told us we had to carry that monster to the very back of the unit. We told the sergeant to go fuck himself and then eat his pistol. Or we would have, if he hadn't had that pistol.

As he looked at us, he realized we probably couldn't carry the damned thing up the stairs, let alone a quarter-mile down the hall. The women's unit warden told him "no problem," and three minutes later, four of the biggest, toughest-looking women I have to this day ever seen in one place came out, hoisted it like it was freaking balsa wood, and marched it into the unit. We marched in behind them, heads bowed in our shame as weaklings, and now terrified of what we were about to get into. Instantly, the pulchritude was upon us.

We began to suspect someone hadn't really thought this through—the women convicts were loose and free in the hallway. As we followed in the wake of the giants and the B-3, lady convicts crossed that wake and took turns touching us, rubbing up against, even kissing us on the cheeks. A couple of 'em grabbed my crotch. In all my early dreams of rock stardom, it never occurred to me that adulation could be scary, but this shit was Jack Nicholson honey-I'm-home stuff.

The back of the unit was a gymnasium, which made the "studio" choice make at least a modicum of sense: It had a great built-in reverb. The terror began to subside as we all contemplated this. It vanished as we contemplated the two female guards assigned to us. They were flat-out gorgeous, both of them. How cruel be thy warden.

We got most of the work done in spite of our constantly (yet furtively) wandering eyes, but we had to make a second trip to Goree to finish the job. This time all the women were locked in their glass-walled tanks, which lined the hallway, front to back. It wasn't as immediately weird and frightening, but the image of every single woman's face pressed up against the glass haunts far past that instant of fear of a strange woman grabbing my nuts.

The warden sold that record at the inmate store just outside the Walls Unit for many years, and, just like with our later contract with London Records, I received no royalties. Great—something else to contemplate. And bitch about.

We never opened for anybody: We co-billed

And do not try to tell me otherwise. That's my fantasy and I'm sticking to it. In the often-conflicting world of fact, we did play first on a lot of shows with folks whose fantasies and realities had come together—folks either on their way to stardom or already on the pedestal. It is also factual that we were asked to perform first at many of these to help the second act draw. In Fantasyland, Cleve didn't just co-bill with him; he *is* Bruce Springsteen. And platinum records line his walls. Fuck facts.

Not many jam bands can lay claim to having co-billed with Al Green. Greezy Wheels can. Al had his monument erected in soul music; our monument was in hippie, Dead-y, trippy shit, and even then it was more of a termite mound than a monument.

The reason we performed together was we had the same lord and master, London Records (Al's Hi Records label was distributed by London). The label had decided to waste some more of our money and bring us to NYC for a showcase at a joint called Reno Sweeney. We were told it was to be a media unveiling or something—both acts had upcoming records—

but I suspected the company just wanted to party down semi-privately with their chattels. The lack of any media in sight and the later bill for fifty-seven grand would confirm my suspicions. Gotta say though: We paid for a helluva party. Fuck you very much, London Records.

We were loved by most of the label people, and our show was well-received, but they were obviously there to see Al Green, who had made them soooo much money. And he delivered, though in a different way than I might have predicted. He and his producer, Willie Mitchell, had brought the studio tracks, sans the lead vocal, for four cuts from the new album. Yup, Al Green did karaoke.

He did undoubtedly the greatest karaoke that has ever been done, and I believe one of the tunes went on to be a top-ten hit. The company went coconuts—some may have lost their minds forever—but at the end of the four songs, there was nothing left. Except the same four songs. He ended up going through the repertoire three full times, by which time I had begun cutting myself. Hey, I love the guy and his music, but the only music I listen to repeatedly is my own hippie, Dead-y, trippy mix.

There was a bonus on this trip to NYC: We got to stay at the Warwick Hotel, where the Beatles had stayed when in the city. We had windows overlooking the avenue, so it was easy to fantasize Beatleness, except that the only people yelling up to us from the street were pleading with us not to moon them.

The real media event for our first record was at the Bottom Line, once the premier showcase club in NYC and later my competitor for talent when I was at the Lone Star Cafe. It was our big record-release party, and we were co-billed with Dr. Hook's Medicine Show. They were just moving up to the east side at *Billboard* magazine with "She's Only Sixteen." We liked these guys—important, since we had to do four nights with them—but I did ponder their lyrical choices for that tune. These guys were in their thirties (and maybe forties).

Unfortunately, we *just* missed breaking it big, way big, with this series of shows. On every night but the first one, we ended our set with Sweet Mary's blistering version of "Orange Blossom Special" and brought down the house. I mean killed it. But it was the first night that counted. All the major press was there that night, primed with champagne by the company drones, all to make us stars. We were set to break into our last two numbers when we were told we only had time for one. I had just put on the guitar I used for the second-to-last song. We ended the set with the set-up song, not the closer. Lesson learned: You have to give it to the closer in the bottom of the ninth if you want *Rolling Stone* to slobber over you.

We totally cheesed Dr. Hook over the next three nights. Blew it up real good. In the end, though, they got the sixteen-year-old, made a ton of money with her. I wonder if they've all finished their sentences. . . .

It's been well-documented over the years that Greezy Wheels opened seminal shows for both Willie Nelson and Springsteen, each time at the behest of Eddie Wilson and Bobby Hedderman at the Armadillo World Headquarters. We were asked to take one for the team and accept about a tenth of what we made in our own usually sold-out shows. We did owe the Armadillo fealty for Eddie having discovered us and taken us from dive to diva. We soldiered up, brought our crowds, and helped make history—in my case, the history of a grumbling old fart has-been who has never come to terms with being second chair in life's orchestra.

One of my personal fave co-bills was with Freddy Fender, whose personality was as sweet as his tenor. Roberto at Liberty Hall in Houston was trying to help Freddy revive a career that had been dormant since he was popped with some weed and served three years in the slam. Freddy and I spoke a language that only ex-cons spoke. Of course, his had just a twist of an accent, like most Texas-born Latinos.

We were absolutely on fire that night, maybe as good a performance as we ever gave, and Freddy knew it. So did the raving audience. Freddy's band was brand-new, not well-rehearsed, and Freddy knew that too. I was almost embarrassed at the heaps of praise Freddy had for us and the profuse apologies for not having given his best performance. I say "almost," because it never really embarrasses me to be lauded. I am one big ego sponge. Freddy became a lifelong friend. I just wish his life had been a little longer.

I cannot honestly say that about the reviewer from the *Houston Chronicle,* a guy named Bob Claypool. Claypool had evidently seen a different show than the one we presented. His review claimed that Freddy blew the Greezy Wheels off the stage that night, that Freddy was an anointed one, and we were a small termite mound at best. Not even a mound. Claypool didn't just body-slam us once; he did it again not too long after this. Brutally, for no other reason than to enjoy the sound of bodies being slammed into canvas.

Several years later, a career of co-bills came home to roost when, while working at the Lone Star, Mort booked Mary and me for a duet at a book-signing. The author was . . . Bob Claypool. I was not the one about to be roosted. I was the rooster. Perseverance furthers. Everlasting joy.

As is often the case with someone in the spotlight, that someone does not always see beyond the klieg lights. Bob was gleefully signing, posing, and totaling up his winnings as Mary and I played. I waited for just the right moment, right after we did one of our signature Greezy Wheels originals. Despite the fact that we were standing behind him, and all I could see was the back of his rather large head (yes, he was a fathead), I could tell that suddenly something was dawning in Bob Claypool's brain—the brain I had previously determined to be much smaller than his head.

"Remember Greezy Wheels, Bob?" The red neck blanched into a nice ivory, and (I swear to you) a bead of sweat dropped from his ear lobe. It was one of the greatest encores we ever received.

Not everyone I've met is good peeps

I would love to tell you that we are all brothers and sisters in a loving global family, that peace and love rules the universe, that we all live harmoniously as a species. Unfortunately, that is such bullshit I can't even believe I just wrote it. The sad truth is we are a species of ill-mannered primates who throw feces at one another on a daily basis. Yes, there are good people everywhere, but there are also chest-thumpers, advantage-takers, liars, miscreants, and the ridiculously privileged among the great apes.

Neither is it easy to discern the difference between a genuinely giving person and a genuine piece of shit. Jeffery Dahmer had adorable dimples. Winston Churchill was one ugly fucking Englishman. One of the most infamous serial killers of the new century, Robert Durst, once looked like a choirboy. I can attest to this because Little Bobby Durst was a regular at Kinky's shows at the Lone Star. He was nothing special at all amongst the cast of characters that inhabited Kinky's hyperspace.

Almost hidden among the JDL members, street freaks, rock-and-roll swindlers, dealers, charlatans, and pimps that circled Kinky like a little Jewish solar system, Bobby Durst was nearly nondescript, albeit in a creepy way. He was no more creepy than anyone else. Except that he *was* creepier because he wasn't as visibly creepy as the others. You had to be pretty fucking creepy to be a part of that planetary group. You simply did not fit if your creepiness lacked depth.

It would not be unreasonable to assume that Bobby may have known this—and been so deeply offended at not being one of the inner planets due to a perceived lack of creepy that he spent the next forty years proving he was the king of creep. I think he did a pretty good job making himself look creepier. I doubt he's getting brotherly love in the joint.

Or maybe he is. It is amazing what you can find in the joint. I managed to find my little niche in convict lore, and so did another guy I met while down there. His name was James Cross. He'd been given eighty years for killing two women and dumping their bodies in a field after keeping them in his closet while he went on a date. You'd think he reached rock bottom with the double homicide. Think again. While serving twenty-seven years out of an eighty-year jolt, he performed the ultimate indignity upon the prison population. He chartered a chapter of the Chamber of Commerce in the Walls Unit and paroled out for good behavior. How fucking creepy is that?

The creepiest convict of all was a guy named Fred Carrasco. My one run-in with Fred happened in the commissary line, the evil punishment one had to endure to get cigarettes and Vienna sausages, two of the most prized commodities in the slam. Carrasco cut in front of me, a huge convict no-no. I was about to strangle him with my belt—I didn't carry a shiv, like most of my compadres—when the guy behind me whispered "not a good idea."

When someone you don't know whispers something like that, you have two lines of thought: He's either partnered up with the offender and about to assault your kidney, or he's merely trying to save that kidney from the offender's freshly sharpened toothbrush. The look on the guy's face said it all: He was as afraid of Carrasco as he was telling me to be. I am very good at following instructions.

My sentence was commuted shortly after this happened, and I walked out on January 18th, 1974. Six months later, word got out of a major prison escape attempt . . . by Fred Carrasco. He and a cohort managed to smuggle a couple pistols in and took hostages in the Walls library, which sat atop the dining hall. They built what they imagined to be a tank out of blackboards and mattresses, forced the unit typing teacher inside with the two of them, and started down the stairs and ramp toward the courtyard, guns ablaze. Soon the mattresses were also ablaze, as every gun in the warden's arsenal opened fire.

I was deeply sorry to hear that the teacher, who had taught me how to hen-peck shit like this, was instantly killed, but I will not say the same for Carrasco and his henchman. They were shot to pieces, Bonnie-and-Clyde style, closed-casket style. Fred deserved it. You simply do not cut lines in prison.

One fun note: One of the most hated young sergeants at the Walls was the only casualty on the Warden's team. He was shot in the ankle as he ran like a terrified rabbit from the action. I forgot to mention: There are just as many pussies as creeps in the joint.

One does not have to kill people to be despicable or . . . icky. You can just be arrogant and thoughtless if ya like. This mostly applies to people who attain something generally non-creepy people cannot imagine—power. Power is the perfect asshole machine. It's part of the plan: You attain it so you can push others around and not be pushed around yourself. As soon as you achieve the overlord position you have dreamed of since your misspent youth, you become impossible. You are an asshole.

It's not the way our forefathers envisioned it, and I don't mean our Washingtonian forefathers. I mean our aboriginal forefathers. In the jungles of New Guinea, power is achieved through pigs and yams, not stolen votes, blind ambition, and treachery. The leader of the tribe is the leader because he raises the most pigs and yams for the village. He simply works the hardest and has the most responsibility; therefore he is the boss. With all those pigs and yams, he does not have time to be an asshole. So, yeah, I'm a pigs-and-yams guy.

In our modern world, men will kill their own children to own the castle. Granted, they nearly always do at least *some* of the work that comes with power, but it's not nearly as hard as sowing, reaping, herding, nurturing, and butchering in a bare-sustenance world on a jungle mountain top. Our leaders have plenty of time to be assholes, and they use their time well.

But the real abusers of power may well be the wives (or husbands, as it were) of the powerful. This is because they get all the trappings without all the responsibilities. They get a free ride to the mountain top without having to answer to anybody. They do not have to temper their personalities. The worst part is they have no clue what has become of them. As with their husband or wife, nobody dares tell them they have become spoiled rotten.

I'm sorry my Republican friends (and I think I may have one or two left), but it was my displeasure to experience all of the above with Laura Bush. As Daniel Johnston sings, "Let me tell you a little story . . ."

Kinky convinced Laura to headline one of the many fundraisers he and I mounted over the years to support Utopia Animal Rescue. It was a high-dollar luncheon, for which we flew in Delbert McClinton, rented a massive ballroom, and wheedled the media endlessly. It was a sell-out, but before we could open the gates, I had to help Laura and her minions set up her PowerPoint presentation, something for which I was not prepared. It took nearly two hours, and I ended up running all over hell and gone fixing this or fetching that. I hate hell-and-gone.

The event went forward smoothly, without a hitch. Kinky sang, Delbert sang, Laura played with her computer and showed pictures of the family dog. After the performances and presentation, Kinky, realizing I hadn't been formally introduced to Laura, walked me over to her table. He told her he wanted to introduce her to the show's producer. Yeah, that guy, the producer who suffered hell-and-gone to make her shit happen right.

Laura was holding her champagne glass as Kinky spoke. She was still holding her champagne glass in her left hand as she raised her right hand in such a way as to suggest I should kiss it, and continued whatever conversation she was having with the woman to her left. She never once looked at me or acknowledged my existence. I'm sorry, but I call asshole on this.

I did learn something though: I confirmed my lifelong distaste for champagne.

The weirdest shows are always the Kinky shows

It's not like Kinky tries for weird, although he's always been a bit of an odd Jewish duck. It's just that he has some very weird friends and fans. A good number of them are quite famous for their weirdness, which doesn't help reality much. With the right combination of Kinky weirdos in the room, normal becomes a theory.

It is scientific fact that some of Kinky's gigs are fantastical, and some are off-the-charts nuts. In the fantastical category is the night at the Cinegrill in the Roosevelt Hotel, when Kinky managed to cajole the most amazing back-up band of all time on stage with him. I don't mean Clapton and Ringo, though both have recorded with Kinky. It's more amazing than that. It's sick amazing. Sick amazing: way better than amazing.

On piano, we had Steve Allen, whom Kinky and I had both met previously—and who performed some hilarious riffs before Kinky's set. On tenor (and very fucking loud) vocal, we had Sam Kinison. Ruth Buzzi laid down some heavy screech, while Richard Belzer hit some nice growl tones. Of course, Kinky grooved out a nice Jewish rhythm. Kinky's nice Jewish rhythm is somewhat like an old black Delta bluesman: The one beats can sometimes be . . . reimagined.

They all sang together on the Kinky/Chinga Chavin classic "I'm Proud to Be an Asshole From El Paso." Also singing along was an audience as full of weird as our super group. Beverly D'Angelo was seen in the back being pretty and tiny (it always surprises me how small most actors and actresses are—must be some sort of Napoleonic/Sarah Bernhardt thing). Sean Penn was bouncing around out there as well. I'm telling ya: Jewish rhythm, even Kinky's, will get your feet moving.

Most impressively, Lou Rawls was sitting stage right. His table was the superstar table, the one that could have been part of the stage. For me, the show was watching Lou react first to Kinky's show, then to the group grope at the end. I'm not sure he liked it. He refused to join the finale. Kinky was later convinced Lou was put off by some of Kinky's lyrics, lyrics that can be thoroughly misunderstood when thoroughly inebriated or tragically weighed down by a chip on one's shoulder. I prefer to believe Lou felt that Kinky already had a growl, and his would be wasted.

Kinky, Sam, Richard, and I ended the evening at On the Rox, long after bars closed. The four of us plus Richard's and Sam's wives and a bartender from the Roosevelt—who seemed to think hanging out with us was her big break—were the only people there. I'm still trying to imagine what kind of a break that would be from Belzer, Kinison, or Friedman.

Sam's and Richard's wives were both very pretty women. Belzer is tall, slender, quite Jew-y, but rather pleasant-looking (and I imagine rather wealthy by now). He and his wife kinda fit together. Sam was one of the oddest-looking humans I've ever seen. No angle of his body had an equal opposite angle. If you were to try to describe it, you might think of . . . an igloo. The only thing he fit physically was, maybe, a kayak.

But his smile was omnipresent, infectious, and ingratiating. I loved everything about the guy. She must have too: They rubbed noses frequently.

One should not wonder how Maui would be the scene of another top-ten-weird Kinky gig. It is, after all, the primal home of Maui Zowie. Zowie makes you do crazy things, like attack food-vending machines, gulp down gallons of coconut juice, and dance suggestive dances at luaus. Hawaii itself is kind of a macadamia Lotusland—surreal like Gauguin, perpetually sanguine. Who knew Maui had mountains, cowboys, and—just put the gun in my mouth—*discos?* I'm telling ya: Zowie makes you do crazy shit.

The gig was high on one of those mountains. I do not recall how I came across this place as I booked the tour, but we knew zip about the joint until we walked in. Oh, the luck: It was an Italian Restaurant that turned into—okay, you may now pull the trigger—a disco at night. It was owned by an adorable gay Jewish couple from Italy. The place was also quite adorable, which meant Kinky hated it. I had visions of espresso cups being thrown at Kinky by an angry throng of where-the-fuck-is-K.C.-and-the-Sunshine-Band mafiosi.

For Kinky's appearance, the owners had created a space between the gnocchi and the glitter and advertised on the local radio station. Kinky's drive-by at the station helped sell just enough tickets to ensure a show and our pay. A nice little group filled much of the dance area—some seated, some swaying to that intoxicating Jewish rhythm. The show went on. After a few songs, I started seeing more and more attractive women filtering into the room. Okay, at least I had something to watch instead of my six or seven hundredth Kinky show. I had lost count after . . . five.

After he gave me my standard intro as his "homosexual lover," Kinky and I exchanged our well-rehearsed quips and patter during the performance. One of Kinky's favorites:

"Say Cleve, can you get me a cup of coffee?"

"Sure, Kinky. How would you like your coffee?"

"Black, like my men."

Maybe four minutes after that line, I felt a hand tenderly brush across my back and go into my jacket pocket. With a room now filled with hot women fixing to hit the dance floor post-Kinkster, I could only assume maybe one had fallen for my gangly goodness and great punch-line set-up voice. It was an ego moment. Then it was a what-the-fuck moment. It was a guy, the owner of the radio station. I extricated myself, explained that Kinky's intro was part of the act, then cringed into a corner. Too bad he wasn't my type: He had a lovely flower in his hair.

Coincidentally, another all-time-strange Kinky show happened on this same run. Our next stop after Maui was Sydney, Australia. This was the beginning of the infamous Kinky/Harry Dean Stanton/Billy Swan tour. The first show was a large hall in Sydney that the boys filled quite nicely. There were many, many levels of odd for this show, marked perhaps best by the guy who came up to me holding a chewed-up, sloppy-wet inch-and-a-half cigar butt like it was a fucking Faberge egg, wanting to know if it truly was Kinky's discard. I had no clue, but I said yeah.

Chewed-up, sloppy-wet inch-and-a-half cigar butts pretty much all look alike, but I didn't see a whole lot of folks smoking Cubans. Something told me the kid would be devastated if he found out it wasn't Kinky's, so I testified in his defense. My testimony gave the butt provenance. I'm good at giving butt provenance. And I can look really sincere, when I do it.

Kinky's show that night was a true masterwork. He had developed a hilarious version of "Waltzing Matilda" just for the trip, and he decided to close the show with it. Making an Australian listen to "Waltzing Matilda" is somewhat like making an American listen to Kate Smith sing "God Bless America" at a punk-rock concert.

The audience booed the first verse. Kinky was nonplussed. He had dissected the lyrics of the tune, feeling he needed to educate his Aussie fans on the true meaning of the song. He stopped mid-song and put forth hysterical definitions for everything from "billabong" to "jumbuck," but when he described the "swagman" as a dangerous serial killer, the entire place fell apart. By the end of the song, a thousand drunk Aussies were singing "Waltzing Matilda" along with Kinky. Goose bumps, I tell ya.

Harry Dean had the second show that night, and while he was on, two Aussie lads came backstage and asked us if we wanted to stick around for a penis contest. Resisting the urge to ask if there would be prizes, I did have to ask what the contest entailed. Was it like a weightlifting thing, a pageant, maybe an IQ test? Would there be a Q&A with the contestants?

It turned out to be a simple test to see whose dick was larger. *Duh,* like all men with large penises don't want to show them off. The way you decide whose is bigger in Australia is to lay them out side by side on the bar of your favorite pub. This is done in full public view so all can see the greater manhood—and one sloppy Aussie can stagger home knowing he's got superior length. He will more than likely be staggering home alone.

At first we thought this strange practice was simply the result of two men looking for love in all the wrong places, but we witnessed penis flops in at least four other bars on that tour. It's no wonder Aussie women think Texas men, the crudest of all Americans, are desirable. They simply don't know better.

I'm told I am a communist

And that may actually be true. Not a Stalinist Communist, mind you, but a Flower Child Communist. The only torture a Flower Child Communist (FCC) will inflict on you is the horror of bogarting a joint, though some will say vegan food is worse than waterboarding. On the latter account, I tend to agree. Mary and I tried vegan for about a year, and lord knows I tried to make that shit taste good. Have you ever *tried* vegan mayonnaise?

A communal lifestyle simply makes sense for a lot of people. Granted, I will not even let my children stay with us more than a couple days anymore, but I have enjoyed the fruits of Flower Child Communism in the past. Yes, there is power in flowers.

The family we had at 408 Cole Street was a functioning commune, except that we lived in a flat in the city and didn't plant shit to eat. This was no kibbutz. I have often wondered why some of my fellow Jews are so anti-Commie. The Jewish state would not have survived without the kibbutz/communal system. Where the fuck would they have gotten their latkes?

Our commune consisted of the equal mix of New Yorkers and Texans about which I spoke earlier. There were three Steves, a Jim, a Colin, and a Cleve from New York, four babes and a guy from Texas, plus a Californian or two to help smooth the batter. We all contributed to make it a slick operation. The Texas gals moved in with state-supplied rent checks, food stamps, and cooking skills, so we didn't need much money to make things work. Good thing. My take from hawking the *Berkeley Barb* "news" rag on Haight Street was about three bucks a day. Until I got the gig at the post office, I covered the avocados.

Like many of the families in the Haight era, we attended big shows together, hung together at those shows, and often slept together after those shows. Occasionally there were mixed "marriages" with other families. My one experience with inter-familial cohabitation did not go so well. The lady in question, whom we picked up hitchhiking on the way to Big Sur, stayed two days, declared an annulment, and stole everyone's money stashes on the way out the door. I should have signed a pre-nup.

One of the best aspects of communal living at flower level is that someone nearly always has a joint to share. This was so very true at 408 Cole Street. If we didn't have one in house, we almost always knew where to find one. Grade A indica was being shipped back by the GIs in Nam in cigarette cartons by the truckload, and one outstanding entrepreneur in Calcutta was flooding the Haight with hashish shipped in tomato cans. We named him businessman of the year.

We had no boss, so all decisions were made jointly—like, would we be attending the Avalon Ballroom that evening or trying out the new-fangled hookah downstairs? Silly question.

Big Rikke probably incited the most mayhem, though her common sense may have saved me one evening when she flat-out ordered me *not* to participate in that evening's family experiment of taking acid and Romilar together. I'm still not sure everyone returned from that journey.

The problem with the commune of the flower child is . . . the flower child. The hippie lifestyle demands that one follow the spirits, decipher auras, and free oneself from worldly bounds. This translates into zoning out, hallucinating, and sloth. If the hippie cannot pay a fair share of the rent, rather than knuckling down to earn the bucks, the hippie splits. The reliability of the flower child is negligible.

The 408 Cole Street communal morphed, adapted, weakened, and finally melted down into a single family flat. The last time I looked, though, there was still a god's eye in the bay window. It says: Communists lived here.

Another form of communism is the extended-family gambit. Many cultures practice this one-for-all concept. Not so much in the U.S., where jokes about cousins begetting circus freaks are still too fresh in our PC memories. I submit that one is not necessarily fucking a cousin, if one is living with a cousin; but yeah, it does happen.

It did *not* happen at 233A Clinton Street, Brooklyn. Not with my family. Through a full series of butt dials, Mary and I ended up sharing a four-story brownstone with my ex, Little Nancy, all three of my kids (two by Nancy, one by Mary), my sis Lissa, my Dad, Stephen Anander and his girlfriend Julie, and our live-in baby sitter, Tammy. Six bedrooms, three baths, full kitchen, plus basement and backyard—all chock full of Hattersleys or related personnel, plus dog and turtle. No cousin fucking.

Nancy was working at Stiff Records, Lissa was working full time and doing the ads for the Lone Star, Mary and I were working yikes hours there, Julie was working crazy hours at SIR, and Stephen . . . well, I have to take my hat off to my old pal: He had mastered the art of gigolo. Dad had mastered the art of manic depression, so he mostly stayed asleep or at Kings County Hospital.

This meant there was no discernible adult overlord (Tammy was just a few years older than Harmony, my oldest). Exactly: *Lord of the Flies*. Who the fuck knew what was going on at the house while the rest for us were earning the rent? All I know is that something changed in the house every time I left for a night's work. One day, magical crayon drawings would appear on the freshly painted bone-white closet doors; the next, the baseball I had Goose sign for my son, Happy, would suddenly be deeply grass-stained with a crudely retraced signature. Happy has a kind of Oriental spirit, in that the true meaning of the ball lay not in the autograph but in its special purpose—being pounded into the dirt repeatedly by Happy.

This commune too dissipated over time, with Nancy deciding to move back to Texas with the kids and Lissa moving into Manhattan. But before we left 233A Clinton, the kids decided to leave their marks at PS 29. All they had to do to was wear their Stiff Records t-shirts to school. These, of course, were the Stiff Records t-shirts that said "If It Ain't Stiff, It Ain't Worth a Fuck." Within thirty minutes, they were sent home for the day. Every fucking one of them expressed shock and dismay. They barely missed shock and awe on their asses.

That was thirty plus years ago, but I'll bet PS 29 still remembers the day the Hattersley clan stiffed 'em.

It was a grand experiment, for sure. The kids had loving parents all around them, even though the parents varied, and had not other butt dials occurred in each of our lives, we could have existed many years together. We all learned something from it, except maybe the turtle—unless one counts discovering too late that it could fit through the outside air-duct grill and fall to its starvation death as learning something.

I guess we should have passed on some of those gigs

It's just really difficult to give up a chance to make enough money to pay your rent. I've spent half a lifetime booking gigs for clubs, the band, for Kinky, for Lou Ann Barton, Chris Duarte, and many others large and small. It's always a stomach-churning, life-as-terra-cotta nightmare. You start with a blank calendar and the knowledge you must fill every fucking date with something. Then you have to take that patchwork miracle you managed to fabricate out of nothing to the artist to get approval for the tour.

In my first year working with Duarte, I put well over three hundred dates on his calendar, and was chided for not having booked all three hundred sixty-five. With Greezy Wheels, the goal for eight years was to try to get five days booked in every week of the year. Kinky's appetite for work, when touring, is legendary. He's an honest-to-gawd Jewish Energizer Bunny, one who hates to pay for a hotel room on a night off. And he rarely has to pay for only one. MC Bunny's got entourage.

So it's pretty much a matter of metrics that some gigs are just not going to go well. As an agent, you merely try to limit the shit storms. You cannot block them out—you can only refuse to return to the scene of the shit.

Sometime it's a paycheck that lures you, a fee much greater than your normal take from a village. Maybe it's a grand opening, or it's a frat party at the local animal house. One to avoid at all costs is the amusement park. We did one of those. Once.

Some barely post-teenaged wannabe, with pocks having just replaced the pimples, caught the Greezy Wheels at Liberty Hall in Houston and told me to call him about a "good gig at Astroworld." This did not sound like our cup of beer. I was about to refuse him when he continued with "it pays a grand." In those days, a grand still had magic. We took the gig.

We regretted it as soon as we got to Astroworld. There was a stage, yes. They had lights, yes. They had sound, yes. They had no audience, WTF? The performance "ride" we were stuck in was set up like a driver's license bureau waiting line: People walked in one door, passed back and forth in front of us three times, and walked out the exit door. We were playing a fucking drive-in restaurant—without the food.

At an amusement park, people want to hit the roller coaster, not the hippie-band ride. Once word got out on the grounds about ours being the worst ride on campus, only folks who didn't want to stand in line for the good rides came through to see us. The impatient, the bored, the fiercely lazy—a typical Greezy audience. See how a grand could put a good spin on just about anything?

High on the list of Jesus-did-we-really-have-to-take-this-one gigs was our first sojourn to Alpine, Texas. Yes, world, there is an Alpine, Texas. It is not Swiss . . . in any way. There are some lower-shelf mountains out there in deep West Texas, and there is some ruggedness to the area, but no snow caps, no yodeling, no men in shorts with suspenders blowing long, penis-shaped alphorns. As far as I know.

Most of the ruggedness comes from the border-patrol meatheads who stop any car that flashes its lights at the cops' perpetually bright headlights, and rampage through local bars looking for illegals. You know: just a bunch of good ole boys having fun.

And yet, adventurers flock to the area, where there are artist enclaves around every corner. For some unfathomable reason, it is also a summer getaway for the rich. Please listen to me: If you are not rich, avoid the summer getaways of the rich at all costs. Combine artist enclave with rich getaway and you get noxious gas. Look it up in your chemistry text.

However, for this gig, we saw none of that. This gig was a supposed festival on a mountain top somewhere outside civilization. We were the headliners, getting the big check. There we go again—the big check. It's always the big check that lures you into the clutches of evil. You never know the shit is hitting the fan until you enter the venue—or in this case, step outside the van into a sandstorm. I may have forgotten to mention how dry West Texas can be.

And it was already chilly in the mid-afternoon. The stage was about the size of a flatbed truck, positioned at one foot above ground level. A sense of doom very often will fill your heart in times like these. This doom was also clogging up our nasal passages with sand and smaller insects.

To say the attendance was less than expected would be

a lie—I didn't expect fucking anybody at this festival—but there were maybe sixty folks in the pit of misery, all told. I had deposited the big check before leaving, so I was okay with the small crowd. We just wanted out of purgatory as quickly as possible. We stayed in the van through three or four sets by local bands, stepping out only to use the luxurious single port-a-can when desperate. I am nearly always the most desperate man.

Dark was settling in and my Greezy mates were growing restless, so I collared the organizer and asked if we could go on before the next act. He said he understood, but asked if, instead, that act did only one song; that poor bastard had been there on the mountain since morning. I agreed, but I begrudged. I am not a pretty person when I start begrudging shit.

I had not yet heard of the person doing the one song—who turned out to be Bobby Bridger. Bobby is a great guy, whom I have known since then and respected to the nth degree forever. He has devoted much of his life to telling the stories of the great Native American tribes and peoples and preserving a part of America so many people want to forget or have never delved. What I did not know at the time was that he had just finished writing and recording his definitive musical history of the Lakota tribe. What I also did not know was that the song was . . . one hour long.

Forgive me, Bobby, but fifteen minutes into that song I went tribal on my own. I hit defcon-one Crazy Horse level, and the guy on stage up the hill was looking mighty Custer. But what are you gonna do? Bobby's story was too close to our family's heart, we being blood brothers/sisters of the Montana Blackfoot tribe through our grandfather. I sheathed my poison-tipped arrows and retreated back to the van—what Custer should have done.

It was maybe fifty-five degrees on the mountain top when we finally did our set. We played everything at Ramones speed and bolted the grounds as soon as we could pack up. The nine-hour drive back to Austin was actually not unpleasant. Sometimes, after a get-me-the-fuck-out-of-here gig, you are so relieved to be on the road, life is good again. Until you get home and discover that the big check bounced. I knew I should have strangled that promoter when I had the chance.

Sad to say, but fifty-five degrees is not the coldest gig we ever played. That award—and it does get the *Clevie* award as worst gig of all time—goes to a protest show we agreed to perform in San Antonio. It was fealty to a promoter friend who'd helped us, and whom we'd helped when possible as well. All I knew was we were protesting a controversial road already under construction. My one concern was that we might have been just a little late with the protest. You know: road already under construction.

We circled through several missed and wrong turns before we found our spot, an unlit intersection of two very remote roads, one of them . . . under construction. There was a giant trashcan bonfire in front of a flatbed truck stage (yes, we have known many flatbed trucks, some biblically) that had two white lights shining on its emptiness. There were no more than twenty or so folks either hanging over or cavorting around the trashcan (hippie gatherings always have a few cavorters). It was forty-three degrees outside. I was hitting two-twelve inside.

No matter what I tried, I could not get our friend to let us out of the deal, which of course was for no check. No check is nearly as bad as a bounced big check, except that your character gets a bonus point for thinking rightly, supporting goodness. There was no playing this set at Ramones speed. At that temperature and wind chill, blood thickens, fingers slow down, the will to sing "May the Circle Be Unbroken" freezes completely.

Twenty minutes later, we lammed it off the stage and away before our friend could stop us. There is only so much right thinking and goodness support in me.

There is a moral in here somewhere. I'm guessing it has to do with big checks and expectations, no checks and expectations, or maybe it's simply all about amusement parks. In West Texas.

Yeah, that's me: ace sideman

I'm not sure how I can make this more clear: NOT. For some reason I wasn't really meant for a life of sit-ins. Yes, I torched Cippolina once, and I occasionally did some nice work with my buddy George Worthmore, but I was never destined to be the grace notes. This is because a great deal of my notes have no grace. Add to this my enormous ego—and that I am remarkably glib—and you understand why band leader was the only option. I am impossible to lead, but I am uncannily graceful in between songs.

I should have known this about myself by the time I asked one of our opening acts at the Lone Star if I could do a couple numbers with her. She was a very young Lucinda Williams. She was also already a very old soul. Mort hadn't told me much about her before I arrived that evening, but her first set told the story. This chick was good, way good. I wanted very much to play with her goodness.

It wasn't like sitting in with Gravenites to show up a guitarist having a really bad night. It was more like sitting in to see if this guitarist could cut it. This guitarist could not.

Lucinda's guitar work was sophisticated, firmly rooted. Mine was open-wound raw, with zero understanding of genre. I did torch a good break on the first cut, a straightforward rhythm-and-blues thing, but I was dog shit when she dug deeper into her repertoire. In those days, if you added a single chord beyond the basics in blues, you were immediately regretting that you allowed me on stage.

Somehow, Lucinda put up with me for two more songs, probably to allow me to thoroughly stink up the place, before I slinked off to the executive dumper to hang myself on a coat rack. Just as I finally began to recover composure and dignity, Mary expressed her extreme displeasure in me having sat in with Lucinda at all. To this day, I cannot tell you if she was jealous—Lucinda was wearing a round-top, flat-brimmed cowboy hat that looked a bit too New Mexico (Mary's from Las Cruces)—or pissed that I stunk up the joint. I'm going to go with jealous, for dignity's sake.

I should have followed the lessons of a few years before. The first occurred at Armadillo World Headquarters, sometime during the Truman administration. The band was still young and raw, especially me. I took young and raw to new levels. Nobody was more infantile than I. Nobody had a redder ass.

For a short time in its history, the Armadillo stage was in the center of the floor, while a new stage was being built, and the old was being converted into table space and a bar. Really glad it was only a brief while: I'm the guy who likes to sit against the back wall of a restaurant to keep an eye on who's coming. It's the gangsta in me.

On one of these nights, halfway through a set, Leon Russell stepped out of the shadows and asked if he could sit in with us. We were of course tres pleased, but I had to point out: no piano. I figured that would be it, Leon would about face, and we'd finish the set. Instead Leon said: "That's okay. I'll just use your guitar." *Huh?*

He'd seen through my charade: I was a mediocre rhythm guitarist. If he was going to jam, he wanted the good shit. I can feel my tail between my legs to this day. Oh the humanity.

Luckily, the jam was uninspired, not nearly as good as what the hundred or so folks there thought they were going to get. I re-took the stage after a long noodle, and played the shit outa that rhythm. I mean I banged it.

Not too long after this, I got booked to back up Doug Kershaw at a long-defunct but beloved Austin joint, Castle Creek. Whoever booked me must have caught the second half of that show, because all Doug ever needed was somebody to bang the shit out of a rhythm while he destroyed good violin bows on his ancient Cajun fiddle.

I did have a leg up on getting the gig: Mary was on the show. Doug was trying to woo Mary, whom I hadn't yet cajoled into marrying me, so they could gondola off to the swamps as the king and queen of Cajun fiddle. Being from the highlands of New Mexico, she knew better than to live in the swamps. Everyone outside of Louisiana or Florida knows better than to live in the swamps.

I started well, pumping out *chuck-a-chucks* like a sten gun, but Doug always likes to take it up a notch, song to song, and sometimes mid-song. Kind of like an old un-schooled bluesman, only hyped on meth and ambition. Bo Diddly at 78 RPM. It didn't take long for my arms to tire, then tingle.

Just as the tingle reached my elbow, Doug turned to me and screamed, "Take it, man."

I took his scream up a notch and hollered back, "Take what . . . man?" And I kept on chuck-a-chucking. For sixteen miserable, never-to-be-forgotten (hopefully never remembered by anyone else) measures, I chucked it. Not a single individual note, no melody, no nothing. At the end of the tune, I considered throwing water on his electric pickup. I reconsidered and went with glib. Stole the show.

I did not steal the show on Lone Star Beer's first-ever (and I believe last-ever) TV show. Seeing as how we'd helped Lone Star up their sales in every club we played, with Pat's song, they did like to include us in stuff, so they put us on a triple bill with Willie and Jimmy Buffett. Believe it or not, we were all perceived to be at about the same level of national celebrity at that time. You wouldn't have known it by Willie's or Buffett's buses, though. When either parked nose to nose with our 1949 Flexible Flyer, Flexie looked like a cockroach, theirs like rocket ships.

There was no script for the show, other than you play, he plays, they play, we all play together. Sounds about right for Seventies Texas television programming. We filmed it on a dude ranch outside Austin, which immediately made me ill at ease. I'd learned long ago that real dude ranches were nothing like Spin and Marty. Except there are always hay bales conveniently placed for singin' and gatherin.'

I don't do singin' and gatherin' all that well. Nor do I do campfires or camping, for that matter. For some people, camping is sleeping out under the stars. For me, camping is sleeping out over the bugs. Turns out, I equally abhor Texas dude ranches. Maybe it's a genetic thing: Our ancestors were never known as farmers or ranchers. We were hatters, generations of non-farmers totally bugged out on mercury fumes. Ten centuries of looney-tunes Hattersleys have followed.

So when the director told us to play together—and "you figure out the songs, y'all"—I was so far out of my element I was a in a new periodic table. I couldn't play basic country spur of the moment (or, as Kinky would say "sperm of the moment"), and neither Willie nor Jimmy did anything remotely basic. Rather than suck for an entire segment for America's viewing audience, I weaseled into a corner on the backside of the bale—still in the picture, mind you, but not with instrument. I'll take the face anytime I can; I choose to reserve my talents for my own upcoming series. . . .

Every musician has a bad jam somewhere in his traveling closet, even Willie, two of which we witnessed. Neither of which was his fault. The first occurred at a taping for another TV show on the campus at SMU in Dallas. I have no recollection for whom we did this, but if there are royalties outstanding, look me up on Facebook. We came on first and played a tight, slick set. We rehearsed four and five times a week when not on the road: Our sets better have been fucking tight.

Willie did not have such a good time of it. His (late) bassist, Bee Spears, was ill, and a sub came in from San Antonio. This was where I first saw the complexity of Willie's songs. The bassist also realized this, but that did not help him. Willie, ever the trooper, slogged through a full set of what would soon become his "Red Headed Stranger" album. The bass player played a full set of something else.

At points like this, it's like watching an accident in slo-mo, especially for one musician watching another. Instead, I chose to watch another kind of felony happening in the back of the theater. Big Rikke and Jim Franklin, house artist at Armadillo World Headquarters and charismatic leader of the cult of the armadillo, were making guacamole . . . with their hands. Oh, the humanity.

Willie survived and has had a bit of a career, although there was that second bad jam Mary and I witnessed. I had gotten one of those early-morning calls from Goose asking if he could bring some of the team down to the Lone Star that evening. I asked how many. Usually it would be him, Nettles, Tommy John, maybe a couple others. This time he said, "All of them. And Willie's with us."

I knew most of them would be bringing their wives. Corna often came with Goose, Sally regularly came with Tommy. I regularly came a cropper with Bill Dick over comping any group of over two, no matter the celebrity. There would be fifty people in this crowd. So of course I said, "Sure."

The limos started arriving just as the weekend country-rock band was kicking off a set. When Willie and his then-wife Connie arrived, Mary and I met them at the door. I got a cursory howdy from Willie, Mary got a huge hug and kiss. It's kind of my life story. I took it out on Connie with a huge hug and a kiss. I think I won this one: Connie is a helluva lot prettier than Wille.

Twenty-five players with wives crammed into the seating at the front of the club, visible to anyone walking by. People immediately started noticing and coming in. Even more people started pushing in, when Willie took the stage within minutes of arriving and started into his repertoire. What came out was awful. This was a full band playing the wrong notes at the wrong time instead of a single bassist. Amazingly, once again Willie, through sheer strength of character (or ganja, as it were), played a full hour-and-a-half set for my Yankee homies.

Everybody went nuts—except for one particular couple who wandered in about halfway through the set. The woman immediately exclaimed: "Look honey, it's Willie Nelson! And, oh my God, those are the New York Yankees!"

She turned to Mary, who worked the door that night and a thousand more for seven years, and asked, "How much to get in?"

Mary told her it was a seven-dollar cover. To which the woman replied, "Oh that's too much. Let's go honey." Try to fix *this* stupid.

Unbeknownst to me until late in the evening, Russell, the house sound weasel, recorded the set on the high-tech board we'd had installed to broadcast shows on WHN radio. He did so without permission, without informing Willie. I was quite proud of him for this.

But I also knew the tape was worthless. The band hadn't hit more than five correct chord changes all night. No amount of magic was going to fix this shit in the mix. I told him to keep his lips zipped—tell no one. Apparently, Russell had no zipper, for the next afternoon, I received a call from someone I knew vaguely in either the music business or the longshoreman's union, who offered me ten grand for the tape, no questions asked. I did have one question, "Are you fucking crazy?"

I turned the recording over to Mort and Bill, who either gave it to Willie to burn or burned it themselves. I believe I saved Willie's career on that night. Yeah, that's how I'm reading this.

Life is a fucking bowl of cherries

Actually, I have just tracked down the original quote on this. It was cherry bombs. Life is a fucking bowl of cherry bombs, a series of shit piles exploding on the path in front of you as you head to your final reward. There are always a couple tasty maraschinos mixed in here and there, but if you want to find them, you really need to keep your eyes open. And shielded. I'm into goggles.

Everything you ever do or that ever happens to you in life happens in a blink. One single blink can change everything. I believe in the concept put forth by Malcolm Gladwell in his book *Blink,* the idea that you will know everything you want or need to know about a person—whether you will like that person or hate that person—in three seconds. A blink. Malcolm Gladwell should have read his own book. After stating his premise on the first page, he followed with an entire book that I had already decided not to read. It took three seconds.

It turns out I've spent my entire life navigating by the blink. For example, take the Wheels' gig in Woodstock at the

Joyous Lake about a hundred years ago. There wasn't much of a crowd there—locals called it the Joyless Fake—four or five small groups and one guy in the back. The guy in the back was Paul Butterfield, who caught a full set. Sadly, when he came up to the stage to say something, I knew within three seconds he was an asshole. I had a little help.

What he said was, "That was a great performance," to which I replied, "Thank you." To which he replied, "Not you, her [pointing to Mary]. The rest of you sucked."

And he walked out. Couple years later I again had to deal with him, this time hosting him at the Lone Star. I decided not to report the findings of my initial blink. Didn't need to. He was still an asshole. I think he already knew.

There are good blinks, there are bad blinks. You just have to pay attention to every blink, answer every butt dial. It's all very yin and yang. You might walk into a magic performance you neither anticipated nor desired to see, but were enchanted by nonetheless. I had no clue who John Hammond III was until he popped up third on the bill at the Fillmore East. When he nonchalant-ed onto the stage in a cream-colored suit and matching panama hat, and played some of the fiercest, most genuine gut blues I'd yet seen, I did not blink for a full thirty minutes.

Here was this white kid, born of extreme privilege, playing as real as real can be. He was not the most facile player, his voice leaned towards croak, but he felt the shit right down to the deep soil. And the guy was a fucking Vanderbilt heir. Blink that shit.

When opportunity knocks, open the fucking door. I always said yes to the crazy duet bookings Mort would throw at Mary and me while I worked for him, because you never knew what kind of a blinking good time—or catastrophe—might be in store. The best of the weird best may have been a party at the home of the owners of Alexanders department stores, an entire floor on the corner of Park Avenue and 72nd Street—easily worth a bajillion dollars today. One entire room was covered in twenty-four-carat gold. I shit you not.

We did not play in that room. My criminal past cloaked me with a kind of psychic stench for years after my incarceration. They likely picked up the scent. The room we did play in was much better, anyway, because it had . . . Julie Newmar in it. And only Julie Newmar. For nearly the entire engagement, we sang, played, and joked with the best Catwoman that ever hissed at Batboy. That is some big-time yang.

Hanging out with Peter Fonda? Pretty yin, if you ask me, though very entertaining. When casting for "Outlaw Blues," his movie with Susan Saint James, snatched up half of Austin for bit roles, Mary and Lissa were cast as Peter's back-up band for a crucial scene. They filmed at the old Soap Creek Saloon, once one of Austin's very best honky-tonks. While they set the stage and the girls up, I somehow ended up in the Winnebago with Peter and my late friend, Alan Phenix. Okay, there was no somehow to it. Alan had some good blow. Blows were exchanged.

Peter was prepping for a scene that required him to . . . act, but he segued into a min-rave about how Hollywood and the public were all wrong about him being a total drugged-out anti-whatever, how he didn't do all that many drugs and was really a rather normal person. The problem with this argument: He kept stopping to ask if Alan had another blast. Where is the yin in this hilarity, you ask? Neither Alan nor I was allowed to speak while he prepared for his scene. What the fuck? We did as much blow as he did. We didn't get to rant?

Okay, I'll admit I have ignored butt dials, usually with the same ratio of good outcomes to disasters as when I do answer the calls. One of my favorite missed chances was my decision not to be involved in a private party Mort booked with the Kennedy clan, to be held at Bloomingdales. The assignment fell to Don Reynolds, our intrepid general manager. I did have to talk with a few of the Kennedys on the phone, but they all sounded alike, very Brahmin, very . . . Kennedy. I couldn't decipher who was who, but I did know the plan. The Lone Star would supply the food, specifically its famed chili. The Kennedys would wear plaid shirts, jeans, and cowboy hats and . . . um . . . do good.

I liked Don Reynolds. He was a good bloke working for a piece of work, but he was not schooled in restaurant. He knew bar, he knew cowboy, and he knew how to crease those jeans, but he didn't know restaurant. He had to figure out how to prepare something like four hundred pounds of chili in the club's tiny galley kitchen. Instead of subbing out to a larger cooking space and cooking it all on the day of the event, he decided to start a week ahead of time, cook it in batches, pour it into giant garbage cans, and freeze it. There were four full cans by week's end. There was also a non-psychic stench developing outside the freezer.

I was the first to open that freezer on D-Day. To my extreme amazement, and even greater amusement, all four "frozen" cans were bubbling up some sort of bile from their deep bellies. Rotting bile, air-choking bile, I-think-I'm-going-to-be-sick bile. None of them had frozen. Don (and Bill Dick, who I believe was secretly directing this fiasco) had miscalculated how long it would take to freeze that much goo in a too-small refrigeration unit.

But the fucking show had to go on. It's like that series of gags that end with "but we made the gig." One must find a way, one must make the gig. Bill made the executive decision: Just heat it up, stir a little extra chili powder into it, and serve it like it is. Bill never ever liked to refund money—which, I'm sure, served him well. Not so good for the Kennedys.

Who freaking LOVED the chili. They ate every last spoonful of it, until their bellies stretched out over their diamond-and-platinum belt buckles. They raised a truckload of money for whatever the fuck, and raved to all their stupidly rich friends about the chili. There were no reports of sickness or death, and Don kept his always-precarious job. I never, ever ate Lone Star Cafe chili again.

Bobby Lee

Elvis Costello

Townes Van Zandt

Harry Dean

Abbie Hoffman

Bill Graham

Ronee Blakley

Billy Joe Shaver

Cleve Hattersley is a member of the Austin Music Hall of Fame with his band Greezy Wheels, which recorded two albums on London Records and served as the de facto house band of the Armadillo World Headquarters in Austin. As such, it filled the hall to herald the arrival of acts unknown locally in their breakout performances—Willie Nelson and Bruce Springsteen. He managed the Lone Star Cafe and the Blue Note Jazz Club in NYC, traveled the world with Kinky Friedman as his Executive Buttboy (official title), and wrote a column for *OUI,* the men's magazine, investigating the strangeness of the cultural landscape. He has hung with New York Yankees greats, partied with the Not Ready for Prime Time Players, and gone bow hunting for feral hogs with Ted Nugent. He now resides in Austin, Texas, with wife Mary and two cats. He writes and manages Yes Publishing Company.

www.ingramcontent.com/pod-product-compliance
Lightning Source LLC
Chambersburg PA
CBHW071159070526
44584CB00019B/2857